Catechetical Off
National Office for World Youth Day 2002

Salt and Light

HANDBOOK

Preparing for World Youth Day 2002 in Toronto

NOVALIS

TWENTY-THIRD PUBLICATIONS
A Division of Bayard MYSTIC, CT 06355

© 2001 Novalis, Saint Paul University, Ottawa, Canada

Cover design and layout: Caroline Gagnon
Cover photograph: Eyewire

Production team: Fr. Serge Comeau, Nicole Durand-Lutzy, Luc Phaneuf, Fr. Robert Richard, Clément Vigneault

Collaboration: Francine Guillemette, FMA, Thomas Rosica, CSB, André Lalach, Michael Fellin

Accompanying bishop: Most Rev. Gilles Cazabon, OMI

Biblical revision: Thomas Rosica, CSB

Translation: Louise Lalonde, Marie-Renée Legare, Pamela Levac, Bertha Madott, Anne Louise Mahoney, Ferdinanda Van Gennip

Business Office:
Novalis
49 Front Street East, 2nd Floor
Toronto, Ontario, Canada
M5E 1B3
Phone: 1-800-387-7164 or (416) 363-3303
Fax: 1-800-204-4140 or (416) 363-9409
E-mail: novalis@interlog.com

ISBN: 2-89507-240-X

Published in the United States by
Twenty-Third Publications
A Division of Bayard
P.O. Box 180, Mystic, CT 06355.
Tel: 1-800-321-0411
Fax: 1-800-572-0788
E-mail: ttpubs@aol.com

U.S. ISBN: 1-58595-203-6

Printed in Canada.

We acknowledge the financial support of the Government of Canada through the Book Publishing Industry Development Program (BPIDP) for our publishing activities.

ACKNOWLEDGMENTS

Special thanks to:

– the many young adults who sent us their inspiring stories about their participation in WYD 2000 in Rome

– the diocesan co-ordinators of youth ministry: Denis Bérubé (Montreal), Nicole Beaudoin (Saint-Hyacinthe), Jean-Paul Pearson (Sherbrooke) and Jean Tailleur (Quebec), as well as their co-workers, who advised the production team

– the Knights of Columbus, the Catholic Women's League and the Canadian Catholic Organization for Development and Peace who, through their generosity, have made the production of this handbook possible.

CONTENTS

A BISHOP SPEAKS TO YOUTH

Young people from all over the world, Pope John Paul II is inviting you to Toronto, Canada, to be part of the 17th World Youth Day (WYD) celebrations from July 23 to 28, 2002.

This event takes on an even greater importance in these times when world peace and our sense of kinship appear so fragile. May the forthcoming WYD generate in you the same compassion for your fellow human beings that filled Jesus Christ. I tell you emphatically: our world needs you.

You have in your hands a Handbook to help you prepare for this WYD. The paths of faith suggested here are inspired by the Pope's message for this occasion. In his message, he speaks to you with that great affection which I know he has for young people.

If you are one of the hundreds of thousands of young adults who will gather soon in Toronto, your Handbook will help you to open your heart to the richness of this event. If you are unable to attend, it will still help you to discover the Gospel of Jesus Christ as an inexhaustible source of good news for our time, as a spring that never runs dry. At any time during your life, long after WYD 2002 is over, you will be able to return to this book and let it guide your steps once again towards the murmuring of that spring.

I wish you a happy "pilgrimage" as you prepare for WYD 2002. As John Paul II said at the beginning of his pontificate: "Do not be afraid!" Start your journey and let the best in yourselves blossom forth. And as the Pope tells you today, echoing the words of Jesus, be "salt of the earth" and "light of the world"!

Most Rev. Gilles Cazabon, OMI
Bishop of Saint-Jérôme

A GUIDE FOR THE SENTINELS OF THE MORNING

A Word from Fr. Thomas Rosica, National Director for WYD 2002

I shall never forget the night of August 19, 2000, in the midst of that sea of humanity gathered in the field of Tor Vergata on the outskirts of Rome. It was the great vigil of World Youth Day 2000, and I witnessed the Successor of Peter beaming with great pride, joy and affection, as he called his young friends by a new name: "morning watchmen." Pope John Paul II wrote about that same moment one year ago, at the close of the Great Jubilee:

> If Christ is presented to young people as he really is, they experience him as an answer that is convincing and they can accept his message, even when it is demanding and bears the mark of the Cross. For this reason, in response to their enthusiasm, I did not hesitate to ask them to make a radical choice of faith and life and present them with a stupendous task: to become "morning watchmen" at the dawn of the millennium (*Novo millenio ineunte,* no. 9)

In his *Message to the Youth of the World for the 17th World Youth Day 2002 in Canada*, Pope John Paul II writes:

> Dear young people, it is up to you to be the watchmen of the morning (cf. *Is* 21:11-12) who announce the coming of the sun who is the Risen Christ! …Our personal encounter with Christ bathes life in new light, sets us on the right path, and sends us out to be his witnesses. This new way of looking at the world and at people, which comes to us from him, leads us more deeply into the mystery of faith, which is not just a collection of theoretical assertions to be accepted and approved by the mind, but an experience to be had, a truth to be lived, the salt and light of all reality.

I am delighted to present *Salt and Light: Preparing for World Youth Day 2002 in Toronto* as a handbook for the journey to World Youth Day 2002. This book is a joint labour of love by the Catechetical Office of the Assembly of Quebec Bishops and the National World Youth Day Office in Toronto. Over the past few months, two teams worked diligently under the wise leadership of Bishop Gilles Cazabon

OMI, Clément Vigneault of the Catechetical Office of the Quebec Bishops in Montreal, and Fr. Serge Comeau of the Catechetical Department of World Youth Day 2002 to prepare this guide for today's young sentinels – the thousands of *watchmen* and *watchwomen* who are preparing for World Youth Day 2002 in Toronto. I also wish to recognize the contribution of Michael Fellin, a young lay teacher and student of theology who has presented the ancient Christian message in a challenging and contemporary fashion to young adults. Finally, without the patience, encouragement and unfailing kindness of Michael O'Hearn, Director General of Novalis in Ottawa, this book would not be a reality today!

This handbook is meant to be a catalyst for young adult ministry in the Church today. World Youth Day 2002 happens to be the pretext and context for the book, yet is also meant for those who cannot make the journey to Toronto in 2002 but who wish to encounter the Lord of history wherever they may be along the way. Through meditations on Sacred Scripture, the writings of Pope John Paul II (especially his *Messages for World Youth Day,* the Apostolic Letter *Novo millennio ineunte,* and the Post-Synodal Exhortation *Ecclesia in America*), the lives of the Blesseds and Saints, and reflections on Baptism, Eucharist and Reconciliation, young people are invited to rekindle their faith in Jesus Christ and their love for the Church so that the salt of baptism will not lose its flavour and the light of faith will not grow dim, but burn ever brighter amidst the surrounding shadows and darkness of our times.

What lies at the heart of the great adventure of World Youth Day 2002 that is sweeping across our country is the radiant person of our Lord and Saviour Jesus Christ, crucified and risen for us, who invites young people to fall in love with him and to discover a Church that is forever young. I sincerely hope and pray that young people in Canada and throughout the whole world will be drawn close to Christ our light as they accept the "stupendous task," vocation and challenge of becoming "morning watchmen" at the dawn of the new millennium.

Fr. Thomas Rosica, C.S.B.
National Director and Chief Executive Officer
World Youth Day 2002

OCTOBER 1, 2001
Feast of St. Thérèse of Lisieux
Doctor of the Church and
One of the Patrons of World Youth Days

MESSAGE
OF THE HOLY FATHER
TO THE YOUTH OF THE WORLD
ON THE OCCASION
OF THE XVIIth WORLD YOUTH DAY

"You are the salt of the earth...
You are the light of the world" (Mt 5:13-14)

Dear Young People!

1. I have vivid memories of the wonderful moments we shared in Rome during the Jubilee of the Year 2000, when you came on pilgrimage to the Tombs of the Apostles Peter and Paul. In long silent lines you passed through the Holy Door and prepared to receive the Sacrament of Reconciliation; then the Evening Vigil and Morning Mass at Tor Vergata were moments of intense spirituality and a deep experience of the Church; with renewed faith, you went home to undertake the mission I entrusted to you: to become, at the dawn of the new millennium, fearless witnesses to the Gospel.

By now World Youth Day has become an important part of your life and of the life of the Church. I invite you therefore to get ready for the seventeenth celebration of this great international event, to be held in Toronto, Canada, in the summer of next year. It will be another chance to meet Christ, to bear witness to his presence in today's society, and to become builders of the "civilization of love and truth."

2. *"You are the salt of the earth... You are the light of the world"* (Mt 5:13-14): this is the theme I have chosen for the next World Youth Day. The images of salt and light used by Jesus are rich in meaning and complement each other. In ancient times, salt and light were seen as essential elements of life.

"You are the salt of the earth...". One of the main functions of salt is to season food, to give it taste and flavour. This image reminds us that, through Baptism, our whole being has been profoundly changed, because it has been "seasoned" with the new life which comes from Christ (cf. *Rom* 6:4). The salt which keeps our Christian identity intact even in a very secularized world is the grace of Baptism. Through Baptism we are re-born. We begin to live *in Christ* and become capable of responding to his call to "offer [our] bodies as a living sacrifice, holy and acceptable to God" (*Rom* 12:1). Writing to the Christians of Rome, Saint Paul urges them to show clearly that their way of living and thinking was different from that of their contemporaries: "Do not be conformed to this world, but be transformed by the renewal of your mind, that you may discern what is the will of God, what is good and pleasing and perfect" (*Rom* 12:2).

For a long time, salt was also used to preserve food. As the salt of the earth, you are called to preserve the faith which you have received and to pass it on intact to others. Your generation is being challenged in a special way to keep safe the deposit of faith (cf. *2 Th* 2:15; *1 Tim* 6:20; *2 Tim* 1:14).

Discover your Christian roots, learn about the Church's history, deepen your knowledge of the spiritual heritage which has been passed on to you, follow in the footsteps of the witnesses and teachers who have gone before you! Only by staying faithful to God's commandments, to the Covenant which Christ sealed with his blood poured out on the Cross, will you be the apostles and witnesses of the new millennium.

It is the nature of human beings, and especially youth, to seek the Absolute, the meaning and fullness of life. Dear young people, do not be content with anything less than the highest ideals! Do not let yourselves be dispirited by those who are disillusioned with life and have grown deaf to the deepest and most authentic desires of their heart. You are right to be disappointed with hollow entertainment and passing fads, and with aiming at too little in life. If you have an ardent desire for the Lord you will steer clear of the mediocrity and conformism so widespread in our society.

3. *"You are the light of the world..."*. For those who first heard Jesus, as for us, the symbol of light evokes the desire for truth and the thirst for the fullness of knowledge which are imprinted deep within every human being.

When the light fades or vanishes altogether, we no longer see things as they really are. In the heart of the night we can feel frightened and insecure, and we impatiently await the coming of the light of dawn. Dear young people, it is up to you to be the watchmen of the morning (cf. *Is* 21:11-12) who announce the coming of the sun who is the Risen Christ!

The light which Jesus speaks of in the Gospel is the light of faith, God's free gift, which enlightens the heart and clarifies the mind. "It is the God who said, 'Let light shine out of darkness', who has shone in our hearts to give the light of the knowledge of the glory of God on the face of Christ" (*2 Cor* 4:6). That is why the words of Jesus explaining his identity and his mission are so important: "I am the light of the world; whoever follows me will not walk in darkness, but will have the light of life" (*Jn* 8:12).

Our personal encounter with Christ bathes life in new light, sets us on the right path, and sends us out to be his witnesses. This new way of looking at the world and at people, which comes to us from him, leads us more deeply into the mystery of faith, which is not just a collection of theoretical assertions to be accepted and approved by the mind, but an experience to be had, a truth to be lived, the salt and light of all reality (cf. *Veritatis Splendor,* 88).

In this secularized age, when many of our contemporaries think and act as if God did not exist or are attracted to irrational forms of religion, it is you, dear young people, who must show that faith is a personal decision which involves your whole life. Let the Gospel be the measure and guide of life's decisions and plans! Then you will be missionaries in all that you do and say, and wherever you work and live you will be signs of God's love, credible witnesses to the loving presence of Jesus Christ. Never forget: "No one lights a lamp and then puts it under a bushel" (*Mt* 5:15)!

Just as salt gives flavour to food and light illumines the darkness, so too holiness gives full meaning to life and makes it reflect God's glory. How many saints, especially young saints, can we count in the Church's history! In their love for God their heroic virtues shone before the world, and so they became models of life which the Church has held up for imitation by all. Let us remember only a few of them: Agnes of Rome, Andrew of Phú Yên, Pedro Calungsod, Josephine Bakhita, Thérèse of Lisieux, Pier Giorgio Frassati, Marcel Callo, Francisco Castelló Aleu or again Kateri Tekakwitha, the young Iroquois called "the Lily of the Mohawks". Through the intercession of this great host of witnesses, may God make you too, dear young people, the saints of the third millennium!

4. Dear friends, it is time to get ready for the Seventeenth World Youth Day. I invite you to read and study the Apostolic Letter *Novo Millennio Ineunte,* which I wrote at the beginning of the year to accompany all Christians on this new stage of the life of the Church and humanity: "A new century, a new millennium are opening in the light of Christ. But not everyone can see this light. Ours is the wonderful and demanding task of becoming its 'reflection'" (No. 54).

Yes, now is the time for mission! In your Dioceses and parishes, in your movements, associations and communities, Christ is calling you. The Church welcomes you and wishes to be your home and your school of communion and prayer. Study the Word of God and let it enlighten your minds and hearts. Draw strength from the sacramental grace of Reconciliation and the Eucharist. Visit the Lord in that "heart to heart" contact that is Eucharistic Adoration. Day after day, you will receive new energy to help you to bring comfort to the suffering and peace to the world. Many people are wounded by life: they are excluded from economic progress, and are without a home, a family, a job; there are people who are lost in a world of false illusions, or have abandoned all hope. By contemplating the light radiant on the face of the Risen Christ, you will learn to live as "children of the light and children of the day" (*1 Th* 5:5), and in this way you will show that "the fruit of light is found in all that is good and right and true" (*Eph* 5:9).

5. Dear young friends, Toronto is waiting for all of you who can make it! In the heart of a multi-cultural and multi-faith city, we shall speak of Christ as the one Saviour and proclaim the universal salvation of which the Church is the sacrament. In response to the pressing invitation of the Lord who ardently desires "that all may be one" (*Jn* 17:11), we shall pray for full communion among Christians in truth and charity.

Come, and make the great avenues of Toronto resound with the joyful tidings that Christ loves every person and brings to fulfilment every trace of goodness, beauty and truth found in the city of man. Come, and tell the world of the happiness you have found in meeting Jesus Christ, of your desire to know him better, of how you are committed to proclaiming the Gospel of salvation to the ends of the earth!

The young people of Canada, together with their Bishops and the civil authorities, are already preparing to welcome you with great warmth and hospitality. For this I thank them all from my heart. May this first World Youth Day of the new millennium bring to everyone a message of faith, hope and love!

My blessing goes with you. And to Mary Mother of the Church I entrust each one of you, your vocation and your mission.

From Castel Gandolfo, 25 July 2001

JOHN PAUL II

INTRODUCTION

Salt and Light

In the world of the Internet, whether we are looking for the Web site of a country or a work of art or a site that will have the answer to a question, there are search engines we can use to guide us along the appropriate path. It is not any different in the vast world of the search for meaning. For young adults of today who are seeking a life ideal that will fulfill them, the Holy Father suggests an unusual search engine. For this great celebration of WYD 2002, he has chosen a saying of Jesus that we do not see often enough on the walls of our cities and in the countrysides:

> ## "You are the salt of the earth...
> ## You are the light of the world"
> (Matthew 5:13-16)

A companion book

In this Handbook, you can outline your own itinerary. Begin with the first path:
- *World Youth Day*: In search of love and truth.

This will get you on track and will help you choose as you go along, from among the seven other themes, the ones that interest you:
- Path 2 – *Hearts in the right place: Being salt and light for our time*
- Path 3 – *Love that transcends time: Jesus and his disciples, yesterday and today*
- Path 4 – *The eye of a needle: Living a moral life*
- Path 5 – *2000 years young: The Church – an everchanging community*
- Path 6 – *Give me a sign!: Prayer, sacraments and celebration*
- Path 7 – *The poor: Our top priority – In search of justice and solidarity*
- Path 8 – *Taking a stand: Being a witness of the Gospel*

In addition to reading the text, do not hesitate to move on to action: at the end of each path you will find courses of action under the heading **Suggested Activities**.

To complement your Handbook, you might wish to keep a notebook or journal in which to write down your own reflections on the themes offered, your answers to the questions asked, and any other memories of the "paths" that you experience.

A facilitation guide

Do you know other young people who would like to travel this road with you through group sharing? To use this Handbook with a group or a team, refer to the **Suggestions for Group Sharing** at the end of each path. You can choose the ones that suit the circumstances and common interests of the group members.

Here are a few "signposts" for your journey. We recommend that you follow them so that the group may fully benefit:

- To prepare for the meeting, read the "path" you have chosen.

- Choose a time and place where the group will not be disturbed.

- Create a climate of reverence at the start of the meeting (a moment of silence, a hymn or a Scripture reading).

- Do a check-in before delving into the topic:

    – How are you feeling right now?

- For the remainder of the discussion, follow the process suggested at the end of the "path" your group has chosen or, better still, adapt this process to suit the group.

- Together, choose the path, date, time and place for your next meeting.

- Conclude each meeting with the prayer for WYD 2002 (page 17).

PRAYER FOR WORLD YOUTH DAY 2002

God our Father,

Your Son Jesus calls us to be salt of the earth

and light for the world.

Let the light of your justice shine in our lives,

so that our words may season the world

with the flavor of the Gospel,

and our lives be shining examples

of Jesus who is the True Light.

We ask this through our Lord Jesus Christ, your Son,

Who lives and reigns with you in the unity of the Holy Spirit,

God for ever and ever.

Amen.

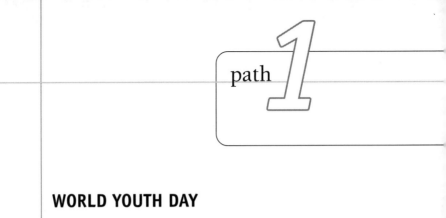

path *1*

WORLD YOUTH DAY

In search of love and truth

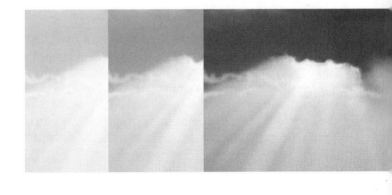

An invitation from John Paul II

I have vivid memories of the wonderful moments we shared in Rome during the Jubilee of the Year 2000, when you came on pilgrimage to the Tombs of the Apostles Peter and Paul.

(…)

I invite you therefore to get ready for the seventeenth celebration of this great international event, to be held in Toronto, Canada, in the summer of next year. It will be another chance to meet Christ, to bear witness to his presence in today's society, and to become builders of the "civilization of love and truth."

(Message of the Holy Father for WYD 2002)

We asked young people who took part in WYD 2000 in Rome to talk to us about their experience:

"WYD gave me the chance to be quiet, to discover myself and to be spiritually nourished. Like so many people, my life is non-stop. That means I am sometimes less able to be truly present to others and to God. It is not always easy to stop and go deep inside myself. (…) Of course, we also had hot weather, long line-ups and crowded subways to deal with. But even these things did not get in the way of my joy. Unlike pleasure, which touches only part of us, joy fills the whole person. I know from experience."

—R.G.

"Every event, every meeting meant something to me. (…) The last few months before I left for Rome was a period of reflection and questioning. I discovered another dimension to my faith. That is what I experienced: a great confirmation. (…) Of course, there are many ways of interpreting a Gospel text, a prayer or a religious doctrine, and we are not all at the same stage of the journey. Nevertheless, many people live out Christ's love in the same way. It was reassuring to see thousands of young people from all over the world gathered together despite their differences."

—G.R.

"I am from Iraq. In Rome I met a few participants from the United States. We had a lot of fun together. You know, we are supposed to be enemies pointing guns at each other, but there was none of that in Rome... Which proves that, when people take the time to get to know one another, traditional feelings of hate can disappear."

—R.L.H.

You will find other testimonies in Appendix B, p. 29.

* What does World Youth Day mean to you?

Life is a pilgrimage

It is often said, and it is true, that WYDs are pilgrimages. But what if life itself were a kind of pilgrimage?

Imagine that you could go on a trip for an indefinite period of time: six months, a year, three years... That you could choose any route you wanted. That you could choose for your trip any purpose you wanted: to have a long vacation, to meet people of different cultures, to complete your education, etc.

Perhaps such a dream seems impossible to you. And yet, in a sense, even without leaving on a trip, we all have the power to make our life a pilgrimage, a "journey of reflection" whose meaning we come to understand a little more clearly each day.

* If someone asked you to describe in a few words your life purpose, how would you reply?

The Bible is also the story of a long pilgrimage: that of an entire people. When, through the Bible, we listen to the experiences of these men and women of another era, we often discover amazing and useful similarities with the lives of women and men today. Bible passages throughout this Handbook will help you shed light on these connections.

WYD: an oasis along the way

On any journey, we need to take a break every so often along the way. This is a kind of oasis, a meal and a bed to renew our strength. That is what World Youth Day offers today's young adults.

It's not that WYDs are luxurious. Makeshift camps and simple meals are typical for thousands of pilgrims. But when it comes to the search for meaning, WYD can become an incredible source of inspiration for the rest of your life. It is like a huge camp filled with a sense of kinship and solidarity. It will be up to you to discover what such an oasis offers you. It is something like an oasis in the desert offers the hot and thirsty traveller, what a good hotel can provide to the exhausted business person, or what the cool water of Jacob's well represented for the weary traveller in the Palestine of Jesus' day.

* Name one or two good reasons for signing up for WYD.

The search for happiness

In his Encyclical Letter *Faith and Reason* [*Fides et Ratio*], John Paul II states that the direction we must give to our lives depends on how we answer the big questions:

> Moreover, a cursory glance at ancient history shows clearly how in different parts of the world, with their different cultures, there arise at the same time the fundamental questions which pervade human life: Who am I? Where have I come from and where am I going? Why is there evil? What is there after this life? These are the questions which we find in the sacred writings of Israel, as also in the Veda and the Avesta; we find them in the writings of Confucius and Lao-Tze, and in the preaching of Tirthankara and Buddha; they appear in the poetry of Homer and in the tragedies of Euripides and Sophocles, as they do in the philosophical writings of Plato and Aristotle. They are questions which have their common source in the quest for meaning which has always compelled the human heart. In fact, the answer given to these questions decides the direction which people seek to give to their lives. (John Paul II, Encyclical Letter *Fides et Ratio*, 1998, no. 1)

A treasure hunt

Everyone wants to be happy. In all our endeavours (work, study, personal relationships, social life), that is always on our minds. Everything brings us back to that simple goal. Let's look more closely at this goal.

We do not always connect our search for happiness with questions about the meaning of life. Isn't it enough to have good health and material things? Or do the roots of happiness go deeper than that?

Let's compare the following approaches to searching for happiness:

The way of suffering

During the Second World War, psychiatrist Viktor Frankl survived the Nazi concentration camps. In a book called *Man's Search for Meaning,* he tells us that those who survived this *hell*, without even having a strong constitution, were those who were able to let themselves suffer. They could do this because their life had a *meaning* that drew them *beyond their suffering* and made them stronger than suffering itself. From this he concluded that, truly, *it is the meaning we give to our life that makes it rich, beautiful and strong.*

The way of restlessness

Young people question things:

I never have time for myself, time to think, to breathe, to put my thoughts and my priorities in order. Everything goes too fast… There's not enough time to live in the present! There is noise, stress, people rushing around, but for what? I really wonder. To make money and buy things? Is that all there is to life? Is there life before death? I want to do something great with my life, make the world a bit better, if I can. Am I the only one having these feelings, these crazy desires?

The way that asks life's big questions

The following words were spoken by Cardinal Jean-Claude Turcotte, Archbishop of Montreal, to a gathering of young people in Paris at WYD 1997:

"What must I do to be happy? What must I do in order not to waste my life and sink into mediocrity? In order not to get stuck in lifestyles that have no future? What must I do so that I may move forward towards greater light? That I may be more loving? That my life may be a song? That it may be a great and beautiful adventure? I hope you ask yourself these questions while looking Jesus straight in the eye and placing total confidence in him, for he is the way, the truth and the life. Do you believe that?"

- Compare these three ways of searching. What do they have in common?

- In which of these three approaches do you recognize yourself most? Why?

Suggested Activities

- Watch the film Magnolia (1999), starring Tom Cruise, William H. Macy, and Julianne Moore.

This film presents the lives of various characters who live in California's San Fernando Valley, alternating among a dying man; his young wife; his son who has disowned him; a police officer who is in love; a gifted child; etc. Through a tangle of comic and dramatic situations, the film creates a mosaic that represents the American way of life. As they grapple with their restlessness, their own solitude and their trials in love, the characters are faced with crises that gradually reveal the hidden side of their being and their obsessive search for meaning.

– How are does this film deal with the themes of faith, conversion and forgiveness? How does this resemble your own world view?

- Ask someone who has already attended a WYD to tell you about this experience.

- If you participated in "Countdown: One year to WYD" in Toronto or in your own area, tell others what it was like for you and what you remember about it.

- Participate in a preparatory walk for WYD 2002, such as the long march from Montreal to Toronto in April 2002 or another pilgrimage of spiritual preparation for WYD.

Open the Bible

One day, Jesus felt the need to rest away from the crowds. But they followed him to a deserted place, where there was nothing to eat. Read the rest of the story carefully. Try to compare the hunger of the crowds that follow Jesus with the search for the "civilization of love" that John Paul II speaks of.

> *When it was evening, the disciples came to him and said, "This is a deserted place, and the hour is now late; send the crowds away so that they may go into the villages and buy food for themselves." Jesus said to them, "They need not go away; you give them something to eat." They replied, "We have nothing here but five loaves and two fish." And he said, "Bring them here to me." Then he ordered the crowds to sit down on the grass. Taking the five loaves and the two fish, he looked up to heaven, and blessed and broke the loaves, and gave them to the disciples, and the disciples gave them to the crowds. And all ate and were filled... (Matthew 14:13-21)*

- If you were asked to replace this bread that Jesus shared with the crowd by an ideal to be shared by all, what would that ideal be?

- Pay special attention to how the disciples acted: how were they able to put themselves at the service of love?

Suggestions for Group Sharing

- At this initial meeting, take the time to welcome one another by introducing yourselves or getting to know each other again. Consider having a pot-luck meal together, with each participant bringing a dish or beverage for the group to share.

- If members of the group play musical instruments, ask them to bring their instruments to the meeting, if possible. (You can do this for any other "Path" in the Handbook as well.)

a) After the welcome, take a brief moment for silence and meditation.

b) If a member of the group has already experienced a WYD, invite that person to talk briefly about the experience (up to 15 minutes). Otherwise, read some of the testimonies found in Appendix B.

c) Have a discussion about the story of the multiplication of the loaves (see "Open the Bible," above).

d) Go through the Handbook together and make an itinerary:

  - What paths would we like to take and in what order?

  - How often do we want to meet?

e) Read aloud the Holy Father's message for World Youth Day 2002 (page 9).

f) If members of the group know the theme song, "Emmanuel," from the 15th WYD (see Appendix C), they could help the other members learn it. This song is available on the CD entitled *ONE*.

g) Close the meeting with the prayer for WYD 2002 (page 17).

h) Choose the path, date, time and place for your next meeting.

APPENDIX A

WYDs: from Rome 2000 to Toronto 2002

John-Paul II shares his experience

Last year, in these very hours, the 15th World Youth Day was drawing to a close with the great gathering at Tor Vergata. I recalled the impressive images of the Vigil on Saturday evening and of the solemn Eucharistic celebration on Sunday, which concluded the meeting. That extraordinary event, in the middle of the Great Jubilee of the Year 2000, is remembered by all, especially by the young people who are protagonists of a promising springtime of hope for the Church and the world. During the Vigil, I entrusted to them with great affection that "At the dawn of the third millennium I see in you the "sentinels"", and the following day, in the homily of the closing Mass, I told them that if they were what they should be, they "would set the whole world ablaze!".

I continue to relive in spirit that intense spiritual event, and I am already thinking of the next world meeting, which will be held in July 2002. It will be another milestone on that winding pilgrimage which began in the World Year of Youth in 1985 and which, from time to time, calls a growing number of participants to gather round the Cross in various places on the five continents. This time we will meet in Toronto, a modern metropolis of Canada in North America, where inhabitants of different origins, cultures and religions live side by side. In this composite and complex reality, the need for Christians to be the "salt of the earth" and the "light of the world" is immediately perceived. Jesus' words: "You are the salt of the earth.... You are the light of the world" (*Mt* 5,13-14) will therefore be the inspiring theme and motif of the next World Youth Day.

> *Mankind in the third millennium needs young people who are strong in faith and generous in serving their brethren. It needs young people who are in love with Christ and his Gospel.*

Dear young people, you understand well that one is not the "salt of the earth" or "light of the world" if one does not aspire to holiness. How I hope that you will never fail to keep this high spiritual ideal in your life! Mankind in the third millennium needs young people who are strong in faith and generous in serving their brethren. It needs young people who are in love with Christ and his Gospel.

The Church points out to you so many of your peers who, in the most varied situations, in our day too know how to fulfil the vocation proper to every baptized person. She shows you the way of prayer and confident recourse to divine help and to Mary's motherly intercession. I entrust the preparation, the expectations and the events of the next World Youth Day to the Blessed Virgin.

Angelus from Castel Gandolfo,
August 19, 2001

APPENDIX B

Young people share their experiences

"The WYDs have been (and will always be) an extraordinary time because they draw us out of our daily routine of *work and study* to re-centre us on this mystery of the incarnation: God is there, I can assure you. I touched him and ate with him. He is Polish, Mauritian, Brazilian. He sings, he gives incredible testimonies, and he laughs…"

—S.F.G.

"One of the things I really appreciated during this pilgrimage was meeeting young people from around the world. I discovered the young and universal church. There was a basic solidarity that united us, as we were all coming to meet the same person, the One who was gathering us together: Jesus Christ. I discovered the Church of Japan and the Church of Korea. I was able to share a common faith with youth from Poland; I met youth who had come from as far away as Kazakhstan, Russia and Africa to express their faith. I was struck by how dynamic the faith of young people from around the world is: it is truly amazing to be evangelized by your peers."

—J.M.

"It was so moving to see that immense crowd and the candles being lit, wave after wave, during the vigil. We were also moved by John Paul II and his very touching sermon: 'In reality, it is Jesus you are seeking when you dream about happiness (…) Dear youth of the century now beginning, by saying yes to Christ, you are saying yes to each of your noblest ideals.' At one point, just like a grandfather, he said to us, quite humorously, 'I don't know what to do, I was supposed to leave at 11 tonight; it's already 10:50 and I haven't even finished my homily…' The applause only increased!"

—R.G.

"It is not easy to organize two million people who have come from the four corners of the earth! What moments of joy and great challenge we experienced! How would harmony and cohesion be achieved in the different groups? (…) The cultural activities and prayer gatherings that brought us together in the afternoon were privileged moments of unity, during which we exchanged and shared with others the richness of our various cultures. For me, this experience was well worth it as it made me grow and everything I learned from others enriched me."

—A.M.A.

"It was magical to be able to talk with others about our faith and live it with people who had come from around the world. We prayed with Italians, Venezuelans, French people, Poles and Germans. The highlight for me was singing the theme song of WYD 2000: 'Emmanuel.' Each time we sang it, all the political and language barriers fell and we could see ourselves reflected in one another through this song. This showed us how solid the Church is and that Jesus truly brings people together."

—N.R.F.

"WYD allowed me to live a very enriching experience, to weave connections with other youth. After WYD, it was time to talk about our experience. So I decided to talk to young people at several schools, in the hope of getting them interested in WYD 2002. Finally, as it appears we are indeed the host diocese for 2002, I think we need to ask ourselves if we could be a host family or a volunteer, like the kind and friendly people of Pesaro."

—J.M.

"The main thing is to taste and sense the universal Church, a church without borders, which is neither white nor black, nor from a particular parish, but which is love and sharing. A church which is both prayer and listening, both sadness and joy. WYD allowed me to taste over and over that great moment of joy and believing. My faith life does not end with the mission in Ecuador or my mission in Quebec; it consists also of daily prayer for all my brothers and sisters throughout the entire world."

—M.B.

"It was my need for God that drove me towards WYD. It was also my desire to live a group experience. To know other people and to live with them. In my group, there was no competitiveness. We were all very different from one another, on different journeys, and we had not really chosen one another. But because we shared one single faith which loves truth, I experienced unity through relationships that were genuine, selfless and not superficial like the world often is. I think I suffer from the individualism of our society, but the Church shows me, through events like this, how beautiful humanity should and will be!"

—P.M.

"In Pesaro, the Italians welcomed me with slices of cake, juice, water… Robin, Salvatore, Charles-André and I stayed with Paolo and his family, who were our hosts. Paolo spoke Italian, of course, but he also spoke English and a little French. Paolo's mother, Olivetta, spoke only Italian. One morning, we made breakfast for Paolo and Olivetta: pancakes with maple syrup. Olivetta found it a little too sweet. That evening, after a great day, I went with my group to a performance put on for all the young people from different countries. (…) We sang 'Frère Jacques' in French, English and Italian. Some people joined in and sang in their own language. It was just incredible, seeing and hearing everyone sing the same song in several different languages."

—N.D.

"We had the chance to talk to Italians, Bosnians, Poles and French people. I found the testimony of the Bosnians very moving. They have lived through war and their lives are very difficult. They find in God the hope of seeing their situation change, the hope of a better life. (…) I came home with a desire to know Jesus Christ better. I am less afraid to affirm my faith. I want to try to change the world a little. I can't do it by myself, but I believe that with Jesus by our sides, if each person pulls their weight, then we really can change the world."

—J.M.

APPENDIX C

Emmanuel (excerpts)

Dall'orizzonte una grande luce
viaggia nella storia
e lungo gli anni ha vinto il buio
facendosi Memoria,
e illuminando la nostra vita
chiaro ci rivela
che non si vive
se non si cerca
la Verità...
... l'Emmanuel

Da mille strade arriviamo a Roma
sui passi della fede,
sentiamo l'eco della Parola
che risuona ancora
da queste mura, da questo cielo
per il mondo intero:
è vivo oggi,
è l'Uomo Vero
Cristo tra noi.

Refrain:

Siamo qui
sotto la stessa luce
sotto la sua croce
cantando ad una voce.
E' l'Emmanuel
Emmanuel, Emmanuel.
E' l'Emmanuel, Emmanuel.

Ce don si grand que Dieu nous a fait
le Christ son Fils unique;
l'humanité renouvelée
par lui est sauvée.
Il est vrai homme, il est vrai Dieu,
il est le pain de vie
qui pour chaque homme
pour tous ses frères
se donne encore,
se donne encore.

This city which has poured out
its life-blood out of love
and has transformed the ancient world
will send us on our way,
by following Christ, together with Peter,
our faith is born again,
the living word
that makes us new
and grows in our hearts.

HEARTS IN THE RIGHT PLACE

Being salt and light
for our time

An invitation from John Paul II

"You are the salt of the earth... You are the light of the world" (Mt 5:13-14): this is the theme I have chosen for the next World Youth Day. The images of salt and light used by Jesus are rich in meaning and complement each other.

(Message of the Holy Father for WYD 2002)

Two real-life stories

Simone Monet

In the mid-twentieth century, Simone Monet was a young member of Catholic Action in Montreal. She was deeply involved in various struggles for democracy, for justice, for truth. Later, with her husband, Michel Chartrand, she never hesitated to stand up for the rights of those who were most neglected by society. She was always at work in the public eye, fighting for many causes: feminist, pacifist, educational, social, church and state.

Simone's Christian faith gave a special flavour to her struggles for justice, just as salt enhances the taste of nature's bounty from the earth. Charity and justice shone forth onto every position she ever took, just as a streetlight guides our footsteps along the road or a campfire warms us on a cold night. In this way Simone was *salt of the earth* and *light of the world*. Her example still inspires women today on their journey towards justice and equality. Her whole life was that of a Christian who was as committed to her neighbours as she was to the heart of the world itself.

Marcel Callo

Marcel Callo was born in Rennes (in Normandy, France) on December 6, 1921. From a very young age, he showed exceptional leadership qualities: first in the Scouting movement, then, when he worked as a printer, at the forefront of the Young Christian Worker movement. During the Nazi occupation of his country in World War II, he helped many of his people to escape, before he himself was deported to a forced labour camp in Germany. Even there he managed to organize religious services and work as a Christian activist among his companions. These daring activities finally led to his imprisonment on April 19, 1944. The inhuman living conditions of prison made him ill: he died at the age of 23 on March 19, 1945. John Paul II declared him "Blessed" on October 4, 1987.

- Try to imagine the many choices that Simone Monet or Marcel Callo must have made to become *salt* and *light* in their milieu.

- Do you know other Christian men and women who offer this image of *salt* and *light* through their lives?

- What choices do you think you might have to make in your life in order to become "salt of the earth" and "light of the world"?

Bringing salt and light to life

Jesus shows us the road to true happiness. But you need to know that this road isn't always fun! We see this challenge in one of the many stories recounted in the Gospels: the conversation between Jesus and "the rich young man." The young man is a decent guy: in fact, he keeps all God's commandments just as they were set out by Moses. Nevertheless, he doesn't think he's ready to follow Jesus just yet, "for he had many possessions" (Matthew 19:16-27).

- What "riches" in my own life would I be most sorry to lose if I chose to "follow Jesus"?

A time to choose

Each of us creates and expresses the meaning of life through choices, based on certain key values. In some way our values become our greatest assets. Values change and grow with us throughout our lives, especially during intense times and moments of crisis. For example, workaholics who find themselves "burned out" might begin to question some of the values that they hold dear. Students whose applications are turned down by the schools of their dreams might have to revise some of their original career goals. A serious illness may lead someone to question everything about the meaning of life, including their spiritual values and even their faith in God.

Using the language of Information Technology, we could say that the values that we cherish are a little like "software" that we install and that then guides us. And because our "software" is alive—not just some sterile piece of machinery—we are often asked to make difficult choices. For example, how should we reconcile our desire to share with others, on the one hand, with our personal need for money? How can we act with respect towards another person while acknowledging our own sexual desires? Our values are sometimes threatened by bugs in the system. To keep our hearts in the right place, to rediscover our inner peace, we have to make choices. Sometimes this may mean changing or upgrading our "software."

• What is my most recent experience with "bugs" interfering with my choices for life?

The key to dealing with bugs

Pope John Paul II lives on the same planet as we do. He understands the difficult choices that underline his call to become, as a follower of Jesus, "salt of the earth and light of the world." Here is an excerpt from his message at the 16th World Youth Day, on April 8, 2001:

> There is a widespread culture of the ephemeral that only attaches value to whatever is pleasing or beautiful, and it would like us to believe that it is necessary to remove the cross in order to be happy. The ideal presented is one of instant success, a fast career, sexuality separated from any sense of responsibility, and ultimately, an existence centred on self affirmation, often bereft of respect for others. Open your eyes and observe well, my dear young people: this is not the road that leads to true life, but it is the path that sinks into death. (…) Jesus leaves us under no illusions.
>
> (*Message of the Holy Father for World Youth Day 2001*)

Life is not a one-way street. Our values – and the choices they lead us to – can make us or break us. There is a fundamental tension in life: one where all those bugs can overwhelm us. As we look at the following cultural stereotypes (and there are others, too), let us try to think more deeply about John Paul II's message for WYD 2001:

- **"To be happy, you need to succeed, you need to achieve your goals":**
  healthy development vs. unhealthy self-absorption

Yes, personal development is an important aspect of human dignity. However, in a culture that over-emphasizes the individual, the search for prestige or for career advancement at any cost takes precedence over personal growth and freedom. In a society obsessed with success, "winners" are treated like gods. This in turn feeds our culture of competition, to the potential detriment of others, our personal health, family life, our need for leisure, and our inner life. In a life where all energy is devoted to the Ego, there is hardly any room left for the salt and the light that Jesus talked about in the Gospels.

- **"To be happy you need to have fun":**
  healthy pleasures vs. illusions

Laughter and love of life are precious gifts, and relaxation and leisure should never be neglected. On the other hand, sometimes we risk becoming slaves to our hobbies or even to our favourite sports teams. Take fitness: when people push too hard, even healthy exercise can become destructive. Take the seduction of lotteries: when empty dreams take over workday reality, we risk losing a lot.

- **"To be happy you need money":**
  financial responsibility vs. selfish materialism

Everyone needs money…especially the poor! But when the lure of wealth becomes more important than our personal well-being and social justice, then we have a serious problem. In the West, for example, the North American way of life and our capitalist heritage have led to the appearance of "the new rich" but also "the new poor." When happiness is equated with material things, then conspicuous consumption becomes the goal of life. How can there be any room left for charity and social justice? (For more on this topic, see Path 7.)

- What is my "top ten" list of personal values?

- Can I identify one or two other cultural stereotypes that sometimes cause bugs?

- What attitudes or habits do I need to work on to make sure my life is more on track with my most treasured values?

Rather than having us look down on our culture and the values of our times, Christian faith can inspire us to dive right into the heart of our world and work to promote values that honour the dignity of the human person. With family and friends, at work or at school, while relaxing and enjoying our leisure activities, through scientific progress and economic development – these are all times and places during which we encounter this challenge of Jesus: "You are the salt of the earth... You are the light of the world."

Suggested Activities

- Watch the film *Dead Poets' Society* (1989), starring Robin Williams and Ethan Hawke.

  English Professor John Keating is passionate about life, and tries to share his enthusiasm with his students: "*Carpe Diem*, kids: seize the day, live in the present moment. Do something special with your life!" Through their interaction with this teacher, the students are changed forever.

– What similarities and differences do you notice between the young people in the movie and young people today?

– What challenges did the ones in the movie face as they took their place in society?

- Outline some plans for a project that will make a positive impact on the world around you, with an emphasis on sharing joy and hope. For example:

– an activity that encourages ecological awareness;

– a neighbourhood celebration or street party;

– a fundraising initiative by your parish;

– a seminar on the culture of consumerism at a college or university;

– your own project.

Open the Bible

One day, while preaching on the mountain, Jesus said:

> **"You are the salt of the earth;**
>
> *but if salt has lost its taste, how can its saltiness be restored? It is no longer good for anything, but is thrown out and trampled under foot.*

> **"You are the light of the world.**
>
> *A city built on a hill cannot be hid. No one after lighting a lamp puts it under the bushel basket, but on the lampstand, and it gives light to all in the house. In the same way, let your light shine before others, so that they may see your good works and give glory to your Father in heaven."* (Matthew 5:13-16)

- Make a list: How was salt used in daily life and in society long ago? How is it used today? (For some helpful hints, see Appendix D: "Biblical commentary on Salt and Light.")

- Make another list: What were and are the many uses of light?

- What is the mission that Jesus has entrusted to his disciples, we who are following in his footsteps? How does this mission flow out of the images of salt and light?

Suggestions for Group Sharing

a) After welcoming the group and taking a moment of silence for prayer, invite everyone to share what they remember about Simone Monet or Marcel Callo.

b) On the theme of John Paul II's message about cultural values (page 38) and the three cultural stereotypes (page 39), identify other stereotypes. Discuss the bugs that these stereotypes sometimes cause in our lives.

c) Read Matthew 5:13-16. One member of the group can prepare in advance a summary of the scriptural commentary from Appendix D.

d) Close with the prayer for WYD 2002 (page17).

e) Choose a path, date, time and place for your next meeting.

APPENDIX D

Biblical commentary on Salt and Light

In every period of history, salt and light have played important roles in daily life. During the time of Jesus, these two images were charged with a very definite symbolism. To understand our calling to be *salt* and *light*, let's take a closer look.

In the Aramaic language, one word was used to signify both "earth" and "clay (that is, earthenware) oven." Instead of using wood to heat an oven (for example, to bake bread), people used a mixture of animal dung and salt. This type of salt (gathered from the shores of the Dead Sea) was very coarse, unlike the fine table salt we use today. Salt was a catalyst that allowed the heating mixture to burn. But after a certain time, the salt would lose this property and would no longer be of any value. That is why Jesus said, "It is no longer good for anything, but is thrown out and trampled under foot." Thus, for Jesus and the people of his time, salt was a chemical agent that helped them to start a fire – to bake bread, to provide warmth, to give light. Now we can better understand the metaphor of salt and its links to light. To be salt of the earth means to be salt used in a clay oven. It means to light a fire within ourselves that will burn away the darkness while helping us to become the light of the world. See how this image of salt helps us understand the challenges of being a disciple: for disciples, too, can lose their commitment unless their faith is constantly renewed.

Throughout the ages, salt has also played a role – hidden but essential – in commerce and industry as well as in ordinary daily life. For example, our ancestors used it to preserve food. Fish was dried and salted over a period of several months before being shipped across the ocean. Also, salt enhances the flavour of our foods.

Jesus invites us to give, like salt does, a special flavour to the world, and to transform it from the inside out. In another parable, he takes the image of yeast, which is mixed into the dough and makes the bread rise. These two images (salt and yeast) are thus related.

Jesus also calls us to be a light for the world, to shine in the darkness.

The image of light has an important place in the Scriptures (Old Testament). Jesus knew these writings intimately. During the creation of the world, God said: "Let there be light"… And God saw that the light was good; and God separated the light from the darkness (Genesis 1:3-4). Later, during the flight from Egypt, God accompanied the Jewish people, travelling ahead of them as a column of cloud during the daytime to signal the route and as a column of fire during the night to light their way (Exodus 13:21). The Psalms often use images of light: "It is you who light my lamp; the LORD, my God, lights up my darkness." (Psalm 18:28) "In your light we see light" (Psalm 36:9).

Likewise, the New Testament constantly uses the theme of light. In the Prologue to his Gospel, John uses the image of light to express the presence of God: "The light shines in the darkness, and the darkness did not overcome it" (John 1:5). Jesus says that he is "the light of the world" (John 9:5). And just as the very first words of the Bible call forth light, so also at the very end, in John's vision of the apocalypse, we read of the light that will illuminate the New Jerusalem: "And there will be no more night; they need no light of lamp or sun, for the Lord God will be their light…" (Revelation 22:5).

Light penetrates darkness. Light makes all things visible. Light spreads warmth. By inviting us to be "light," Jesus invites us to make him present in the world. The Church today has the very same mission that Jesus had: to bring the Good News to the poor; to tell prisoners that they are free; to show blind people that they can see; to lead the oppressed to freedom (Luke 4:18). Sharing this Good News with our brothers and sisters is exactly what Jesus is asking us to do when he calls us to be the light of the world, a light that will shine for all.

LOVE THAT TRANSCENDS TIME

Jesus and his disciples,
yesterday and today

An invitation from John Paul II

Our personal encounter with Christ bathes life in new light, sets us on the right path, and sends us out to be his witnesses.

(Message of the Holy Father for WYD 2002)

During an interview following WYD 2000 in Rome, one young man talked about something important that happened to him while he was working as a missionary in Peru for six months:

"A volunteer asked me to help her bathe and give medical treatment to a man who had been living on the streets and eating mostly garbage. To help this man, who seemed like a piece of 'human garbage' himself, was the hardest thing I've ever done. I did not want to face my own disgust and my powerlessness at seeing him in this terrible condition. But when the moment came for me to bandage his infected sores, I did it willingly and looked him in the eye. At that moment, tears filled *my* eyes and my heart was filled with peace and an indescribable joy. I can't really explain it...God lived in the heart of that suffering and vulnerable man."
—P.B.

- Think about a time when you met God through another person. How did this encounter change you?

- Have any of your friends ever shared a similar experience with you? What was it?

Meaningful experiences

Any encounter with God gives a particular colour to life. Nothing will ever be quite the same again! The Bible gives many examples of men and women whose lives took a different direction after such an encounter. Here, in a few words, are some of the great moments in our "History of Salvation"...moments that are found from cover to cover in the Bible.

A promise

Let's start with Moses, a shepherd who encountered God and then was filled with the desire to free his people from slavery. The source of his strength was a Promise, a special Word heard deep in his heart: *I am with you always*, a phrase that symbolizes personal relationship. This experience of the Divine Presence, intimate but indescribable, allowed him to take a chance on freedom. The same thing happened to King David, through his deeply human experiences of life, as he discovered the many different aspects of God's love. Then there were the Prophets, who gave hope to the Jewish people by reminding them over and over again of this Promise made to Moses: a promise that transcends time.

A human face

The Jewish people often lost hope. During the time of Exile, far from their homeland and their Temple, they felt powerless. They asked themselves hard questions: Has God abandoned us? Will we ever return to Israel? What are we doing here on earth? God spoke to them through the voices of the teachers and the prophets, who reminded them of the Promise once made to Moses.

During the Roman occupation, the people began to dream of a kingdom of justice and peace. Could they dare to hope? Then, one night, the Word of God became flesh and began to show people a new way to love one another. Jesus was born in obscurity. His mother, Mary, was an ordinary woman; his father, Joseph, a simple carpenter. God had kept this promise: to come, to be with all people, to live with us today.

The Word

Jesus began his ministry by choosing his disciples. Together, on the roads of Galilee, they set about listening to Jesus, watching him, questioning him, astonished to see him breaking taboos and upsetting some of the conventions of his time. Among those who met Jesus, many experienced his all-powerful love, recognizing him as the long-awaited Messiah. Others did not. But the disciples, little by little, through their personal experiences of him, learned how to make God's grace come alive in their daily lives.

For the authorities of the time, however, Jesus was an impostor, someone who turned the established rules upside down, bringing their whole social structure into danger. But Jesus was not a fraud. He saw clearly – and listened to his critics. He continued with his mission, and promised his disciples that he would never leave them alone. Right up until the end, he continued, convinced of the truth of his mission, even when it took him into the Garden of Gethsemane. There, overcome with sadness, he prayed to his Father, asking to be spared this final test. On the cross, again he cried out his Father's name, and gave himself back to God as a gift of love. And then, as the women discovered on Easter morning, Jesus rose from the dead!

- Have you ever had an experience of meeting God? Have you ever had an experience that made you question the very existence of God? What were they?

- On what do you base your faith in God?

A breath

It's easy to imagine the disciples' confusion after Jesus died. They gathered together to cheer each other up; to share their memories of him; to talk about the One who had turned their lives upside down. No doubt they were also afraid. Afraid of being arrested and put to death just as their Teacher and Friend had been. Huddled together, they prayed, listened to the words of Scripture and celebrated the memory of Jesus. Still, something was missing: the spark of inspiration to get them back on track, preaching the Kingdom. Until that day when a holy Fire empowered them, filling them with its own Breath and Spirit, the day of Pentecost. And then their tongues were loosened beyond all understanding, and they were now ready to live as disciples of Jesus. They were no longer alone: Jesus had kept his promise to be with them forever, to the end of time.

- In our society, what are the fears that keep our hands tied and our mouths closed?

- What Breath of the Spirit are you hoping to find through your participation in WYD?

Today's disciples

Jesus has now been continuing his earthly journey for 2000 years. During that time, many people have strived to live as his disciples. Some of the more famous ones include Jean Vanier, Mother Teresa of Calcutta, and Oscar Romero. Many others remain unknown. What do his disciples do today?

– some volunteer to work with people with AIDS;

– teenagers regularly visit senior citizens;

– a homebound person writes letters to prisoners;

– neighbours form groups to read and study the Scriptures;

– parents do their best to raise their children;

– citizens undertake urban renewal projects for their neighbourhoods;

– those who have enough to spare give time and money to help the homeless;

– peace activists lobby against violence;

– some retired people drive others to medical appointments or deliver Meals on Wheels;

– women organize to gain recognition of their dignity.

With the Spirit alive within them, these modern-day disciples go everywhere, transforming and humanizing the world little by little. What do all these disciples have in common? The belief that Jesus died and rose again.

They opened their eyes...

These disciples find that they can't run away from the truth, look at life through rose-coloured glasses or make light of our problems. Newspapers, television, radio, meetings with others or walks through town keep their eyes open. They see people in need, like those Jesus met on the roads of Galilee. These glimpses of those around them help them to see their own vulnerability; to recognize their many gifts; and to renew their faith, the faith that Jesus showed his whole life.

- Who are the individuals or groups in your area who are calling out for help? Where are they? What are their living conditions like?

- What volunteer organization could you join in order to help these people?

They watched...

The disciples of Jesus didn't judge, condemn, or act superior. Rather, because they were filled with the love of God, they looked at the world around them with gentle compassion. They wrote letters to those in prison: not to preach at them, but simply to strengthen their courage, to keep them from falling into despair. With this same compassion, Jesus had invited his disciples to love one another, to accept their own limitations. That is not easy to do!

- How do you look at the less fortunate around you that you identified earlier?

- How do you look at yourself?

They acted...

They didn't make speeches; they didn't sit and argue; they didn't issue warnings. Instead, the disciples got right down to business. Each in his or her own way gave a helping hand to someone else and worked to find solutions to problems. Some began by preaching in public about the evils around them. Others worked to improve individual lives and hearts. They all worked according to their own talents. The important thing was simply to get started. Jesus invited his disciples to live in the truth and to fight against any hypocrisy in their own lives as he had once done with the Pharisees.

- What sort of action is best suited to your talents and personal preferences?

- In your immediate circle, what kinds of hypocrisy exist?

They continued to fight…

The disciples kept going in spite of fatigue and setbacks; in spite of the feeling that they weren't making any progress; in spite of doubts about their own abilities. "Keeping the faith" is hard work, but the Word of God gave them a way to begin and a way to keep going.

- What tools (habits, attitudes) do you have that can keep you on the right course?

They found nourishment in a Promise…

"I will be with you always." These words, originally spoken to Moses and repeated by Jesus, nourished the lives of the disciples. The Presence of God gives meaning, brings happiness and inspires action.

People here and in other parts of the world witness to Jesus. Some have been officially declared "saints." But when John Paul II spoke to the young people gathered in Rome for WYD 2000, he dared to say: "Young people of every continent, do not be afraid to be the saints of the new millennium!"

- What does this mean to you?
- In your own words, how would you explain what it means to be a saint? In what ways can we be disciples of Jesus today?

First a disciple, now a saint: Therese of Lisieux

Therese Martin was born on January 2, 1873, in France. After their mother died, her two older sisters, Pauline and Marie, entered the Carmelite convent of Lisieux. These losses plunged young Therese into an emotional illness from which she was miraculously cured by the "Smiling Virgin" Mary. Early on, Therese dreamed of becoming a Carmelite nun like her sisters. Her determination led to her being admitted at age 15. She took the name "Saint Therese of the Child Jesus and the Holy Face." The early days were difficult ones; she discovered the challenges of contemplative prayer and the austerity of the convent Rule. Beginning in 1894, she began to write her spiritual autobiography. In doing so she became aware of the Lord's mercy but also of her "littleness" before him. Thus was born her "little way," a path of trust and giving over of oneself to the mercy and love of Jesus.

When she was diagnosed with tuberculosis in 1896, Therese began "a dark night of the soul" – a time of great spiritual darkness and discouragement. And yet, her willingness to give continued: she always offered to do the least enjoyable tasks, which for her was a way to be "salt and light" in her community. As she faced death, she wrote, "I'm not really going to die. I'm just entering into another life." She died on September 30, 1897, after suffering much agony. During this time of suffering she said, "I feel as if my mission is about to begin... I want to spend Eternity in Heaven doing good here on earth." One year after her death, her spiritual autobiography was published and was a great international success. Although she was almost unknown when she was buried, her grave became a pilgrimage site and reports of miracles soon appeared. Beatified in 1923 and canonized in 1925, Therese was also named "Patron of the Missions."

At WYD 1997 in Paris, John Paul II announced that he would name Therese "Doctor of the Universal Church" because of the depth of her spiritual writings. In 2001, the visit of the reliquary of Therese de Lisieux to Canada coincided with the visit of the World Youth Day cross. As one of the nine young saints named as Patrons of WYD 2002 in Toronto, Therese calls us to trust in the love and mercy of the Lord. "My vocation, it is love!" she said after much thought about the meaning of her life. From inside her cloister walls, Therese sent her prayer out to missionaries, atheists, and prisoners. She found a way to live out all vocations through loving according to her "little way."

Today we need Therese as Doctor of God's mercy because she is someone who lived in the same world that we live in, a world of science and technology, in which a huge percentage of people do not believe in God or at least do not accept Jesus' claim to be Lord of the universe. Therese speaks to us in the here and now of this awesome moment in history. She struggled with so many of the same questions that young people struggle with today: her own faith was under siege for the last year and a half of her life. She loved atheists and longed to give them the comfort of the Gospel. In the last days of her life she was strongly tempted to commit suicide and confessed to surprise that more people in pain and distress do not destroy themselves, especially if they do not believe in God. We need someone like Therese in whom we can see ourselves, with our poor human weakness and all the anxiety and panic attacks that many of us endure.

There is another way to consider her title of "Doctor." It is not Therese who needs it but us. Doctors first and foremost heal the sick, the broken, the wounded. We need to be healed by Therese and her little way of love and mercy. By placing her in the Doctor's chair and putting on her shoulders the Doctor's gown, the church calls us all to sit at the feet of this astonishing young woman, to reread the pages of the Gospel and to be filled anew with its light, so that we may truly become salt of the earth and light of the world. St. Therese of Lisieux, Little Flower, Doctor of the Church, patroness of World Youth Day, heal us and pray for us, as you spend your heaven doing good on earth.

Suggested Activities

* Meet with someone whom you recognize to be a disciple of Jesus.

* Watch a film that illustrates the impact that the disciples of Jesus can have on their surroundings; for example, *Brother Sun, Sister Moon*; *Black Robe*; *The Mission*; *Dead Man Walking*.

* Make a list of the changes that you could make, little by little, in your own surroundings, like Jesus' disciples did.

Open the Bible

Then Jesus told his disciples, *"If any want to become my followers, let them deny themselves and take up their cross and follow me. For those who want to save their life will lose it, and those who lose their life for my sake will find it. For what will it profit them if they gain the whole world but forfeit their life? Or what will they give in return for their life?"* (Matthew 16:24-26)

- How does this invitation make you feel?

Suggestions for Group Sharing

a) After a welcoming introduction and a moment of silence for prayer, read individually the section "Meaningful Experiences" in this Path. Share your thoughts with each other:

- What do these passages teach you about the life of a disciple?
- What feelings surface within you when you are confronted with this kind of challenge?

b) Invite each member of the group to share the name of his or her favourite saint and to explain how the life of this great witness to faith can be an inspiration to us today.

c) Prepare one of the activities suggested earlier in this Path, or choose a different one. If you cannot complete the activity during your meeting, make plans to finish it at another time.

d) End the discussion with the prayer for WYD 2002 (page 17).

e) Choose the path, date, time and place for your next meeting.

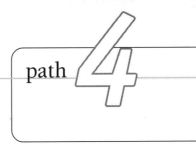

path 4

THE EYE OF A NEEDLE

Living a moral life

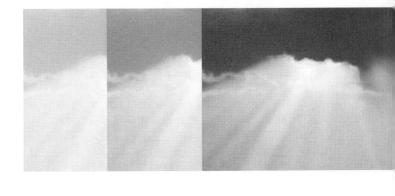

An invitation from John Paul II

> It is the nature of human beings, and especially youth, to seek the Absolute, the meaning and fullness of life. Dear young people, do not be content with anything less than the highest ideals!
>
> *(Message of the Holy Father for WYD 2002)*

One day, Jesus said to his disciples that it is harder for a rich person to get into heaven than it is for a camel to pass through the eye of a needle! (The "eye of the needle" refers to the narrow passageway that was cut into the high walls surrounding ancient villages, allowing people to go in and out.)

The Gospel is demanding: we are called to consider the "Absolute." Gospel texts also quench our thirst for the infinite: don't we all want to love and be loved infinitely? At the same time, we are called to take a closer look at our lives. A participant in WYD 2000 considers these questions:

> "[In my life] I sometimes had a hard time seeing love in the radical demands of Christianity. (…) There seemed to be such a difference between what people preached and how they lived their lives; between the beatitude 'Blessed are the poor' and the lifestyles our society values (…) These contrasts bothered me and I forced myself to ask difficult questions because I was afraid that otherwise I would live during the week forgetting what I had heard at church on Sunday."
> —E.M.

• What do you think of this testimony?

What the Gospel asks of us

The Gospel asks us to be always vigilant, as the quote above points out. It is so easy to be inconsistent. We want to love, but we get caught up in our own interests. We're afraid to take action against injustice. We give up on friendships as soon as things get difficult. We say hurtful words. Jesus knows our limitations very well: he ate with sinners; he went to Zacchaeus' house. He doesn't speak to "perfect" people, but to each and every one of us. We are called to make a difference in our own lives and the lives of those around us every day. Can we do it? How?

Three points of reference

The choices Jesus made throughout his lifetime can help us when we have difficult decisions to make in our own lives. We must consider three things: freedom, conscience and responsibility. Without these three points of reference, no law or moral lifestyle can last.

Freedom

We are born with a lot of baggage: talents, limitations, personality traits, physical appearance and other characteristics. Our education marks us, as does the milieu we grow up in. Despite all of this, there is still room for us to become the people we want to be. We have freedom of choice; the decision is ours to make.

What about the laws in our society? Are they just rules that take away our personal freedom? What about the Ten Commandments?

Imagine a society with no laws. Anarchy would reign, followed by a slew of dangers, including the exploitation of the weakest members. Laws offer us freedom. They tell us how to act in order to respect our mutual rights. God's commandments are the same. In the desert, the Jewish people learned how to keep a Covenant with God and create a society. Here is how one of the brothers from Taizé, a community in France, described freedom to a large gathering of young people in the summer of 1999:

> "God doesn't want to limit our freedom. Instead, he wants to offer us a greater space in which to move. (…) So, when the Ten Commandments say: 'You shall not kill…' they also say: 'You shall encourage life; you shall give life more space in which to grow.' We tend to see the Ten Commandments as limiting. But the opposite is true!"
> ("The Covenant," Encounters of Taizé, Summer 1999)

- How do you react to laws?
- How do you reconcile your personal freedom and society's laws?

Conscience

"Open your eyes! Wake up!" we say to others sometimes. These expressions make us think of our conscience, that capacity we have to look inside ourselves, to make judgments about what we do, to make choices, to open ourselves up to reality and to others. Our conscience keeps our eyes open and our ears tuned to the world.

Our conscience works continuously because we are constantly confronted with new situations. Cloning, for example, was first a possible cure for disease; now it raises serious questions about respecting life. What should we think about issues like these?

It is important to keep informed (to read the newspaper, listen to experts, have discussions with many different people) and to consider things in light of our fundamental choice – our faith in God. In the Encyclical Letter *Evangelium Vitae* [The Gospel of Life], John Paul II talks about the choices our conscience calls us to make.

> In our present social context, marked by a dramatic struggle between the "culture of life" and the "culture of death," there is need to *develop a deep critical sense,* capable of discerning true values and authentic needs. (John Paul II, Encyclical Letter *Evangelium Vitae,* 1995, no. 95)

- When you have to make a decision, what methods do you use to see your choices more clearly?
- Can you give an example of how your faith in God allows you to make decisions more clearly?

Responsibility

Even as children we hear the word "responsibility" over and over. Sometimes we get sick of hearing it! Nonetheless, responsibility goes hand in hand with independence, which is something we all long for. Young adults have a great responsibility towards themselves and others. You have to develop your talents, invest in friendships and loving relationships, express your needs, solve problems that affect your happiness, respect human rights, figure out where your life is going, be true to yourself, stay in touch with God, share and nurture your faith, and more.

Pope John Paul II reminds us of the responsibility Jesus gave to his disciples:

> In our service of [love], *we must be inspired and distinguished by a specific attitude:* we must care for the other as a person for whom God has made us responsible. As disciples of Jesus, we are called to become neighbours to everyone... (John Paul II, *Evangelium Vitae*, 1995, no. 87)

- What does "being a responsible person" mean to you?
- Give an example of a time when you had to be "responsible."

Signposts

In life we are often faced with situations that require us to "discern," to decide which action to take in order to keep thriving and building a world filled with justice and peace. It isn't always easy! The Gospel gives us tools, or signposts, to help guide us on our way. These signposts are the different aspects of Jesus' commandment to love one another:

> *"This is my commandment, that you love one another as I have loved you. No one has greater love than this, to lay down one's life for one's friends."* (John 15:12-13)

> *"Love your enemies and pray for those who persecute you, so that you may be children of your Father in heaven..."* (Matthew 5:44-45)

Read about the following experiences that young adults of today have lived through. They are paired with brief excerpts from the lives of the blessed or of the saints. When you read these lines, try to find signposts that can help you find your way through life.

Compassion

Eva's pilgrimage was more than just a time to reflect on the ways Jesus tells us to love – it was a call to action. She talks about when she and her group were in Rome and met a group of Polish young people who, because of problems and delays on their trip, had not had anything to eat since the night before: "We gave them the rest of our bread... Through these little inconveniences, God allows me to experience the words of the Apostle Paul: 'Love endures all things'" (1 Corinthians 13:7).

Joséphine Bakhita (Sudan, 1869 – Italy, 1947) was born in Sudan. She was kidnapped by slave traders and purchased by a diplomat who brought her to Italy, where she was entrusted to the Sisters of the Catechumenate in Venice. She decided to become a member of the Sisters of the Madeleine Institute of Canossa. She worked with the poor, who nicknamed her "Black Mother." She was beatified in 1992 and canonized in 2000. She is the patron saint of Sudan.

*   How has compassion (the capacity to suffer with another) influenced your life?

Service

For months, Martin has been living in a home for people with AIDS. He is only 32 years old and his life is nearly over. Many people have given up on him for a lot of "good" reasons, but not Charles. He continues to visit Martin, reading to him and keeping him informed of current events. He does errands for him, washes his clothes and makes sure Martin is comfortable in his chair. Often he just sits there quietly and lets Martin sleep. People tell Charles to take care of himself; that he can't do any more for Martin; that he shouldn't let himself get sick.

Andrew, from Phu Yen (Vietnam, 1624–1644), became a martyr for his faith. Born to a poor mother in the province of Phu Yen, he went on to study with the Jesuits and was baptized when he was 17 years old. He became a catechist and evangelized with zeal, filled with the love of God and wanting salvation for everyone. In 1644, he was captured by soldiers in the name of the king, who wanted to rid the kingdom of Christianity. On July 26, 1644, he was decapitated as he cried out, "Jesus!" An inspiration to Vietnamese catechists, he was beatified in Rome by John Paul II on March 5, 2000.

*   Where am I called to serve others in my life?

The gift of self

John and Diane were joyfully awaiting the arrival of their first child. But during the birth, the baby didn't get quite enough oxygen. It was only a matter of seconds, but Samuel's life was changed forever. He is a different child, with developmental delays significant enough to keep him from fitting in with other children. Just a few seconds, but John and Diane will always have to fight for their son to find a place for him in a society that is so focused on achievement. Despite it all, or perhaps because of it all, Samuel is a ray of sunshine for his parents. They were not expecting that, either.

Gianna Beretta Molla (Italy, 1922–1962) sacrificed her life so her daughter could live. Born in Italy, she studied medicine and surgery and went on to open a medical clinic specializing in pediatrics. She referred to her medical practice as her "mission" and took special care of mothers and children, the elderly and the poor. She was also involved in Catholic Action, working with the very young. In 1961, when she was two months pregnant, it was discovered that she had a tumour. An operation could save her, but she would lose her child. She decided against the operation, thereby sacrificing her own life. She was beatified in Rome on April 24, 1994, by John Paul II, who said that her sacrifice was a "hymn to life."

To learn more about the life and witness of Gianna Beretta Molla, read her story in Appendix E.

* How is the gift of self a signpost for you?

Forgiveness

Two young university students, Michelle and Martin, were working as research assistants on a study about respecting the rights of others. They received a small salary and were promised that their names would be published in the study. When the document appeared, only the professor's name was there. They felt betrayed and angry. They felt as if their work had been stolen from them, or discounted. Several months later, the two research assistants met with the professor, brought everything out into the open, and were able to forgive the injustice.

Francisco Castello i Aleu (Spain): Two hundred and thirty-three martyrs – priests, religious and lay people – died for their faith in the religious persecution surrounding the Spanish Civil War, from 1936 to 1939. They all forgave their executioners. One of these people was 22-year-old Francisco Castello i Aleu, a chemist and a member of Catholic Action. In full awareness of the seriousness of the situation, he did not run and hide, but gave his youth as an offering of love for God and his brothers and sisters. Pope John Paul II beatified these 233 martyrs on March 11, 2001.

• People say that it is liberating to forgive. Where in your life do you need to give or receive forgiveness?

Suggested Activities

• Try to imagine that you are the following people:

Lauren and Carina are two young adults. They work for minimum wage at a teen centre in a poor part of town. They need help to keep offering the same level of services to the young people who use the centre. The needs are great, but money is in short supply. When they make their recommendation to the Administrative Council about hiring another person to work with them, they are told that they must choose between meeting the teens' needs and getting a bigger salary for themselves. What should they do?

One day, as Robert was walking down the street, he saw a little boy in tears. The boy's mother was nearby, sitting on some steps, but she was crying, too. Robert wondered what was going on. He was concerned, but felt that it was none of his business. So he kept walking. For the rest of the evening he kept thinking about what he had seen, and about the Gospel. Robert is a priest; he couldn't forget the parable of the Good Samaritan, who stopped to help a stranger who was injured and bleeding, someone whom a Jewish priest and a Levite had walked right by without helping (Luke 10:29-37). Robert can't shake the bad feeling that he didn't know what to do in that situation.

- What would you do if you were Lauren, Carina or Robert? What is your decision based on?

- Reread the quote from John Paul II found at the beginning of this Path. Describe your "highest ideal." Share it with someone else if you wish.
- Watch the movie Keeping the Faith (2000), starring Ben Stiller, Edward Norton and Jenna Elfman.

> In this story, two childhood friends – a Jewish rabbi and a Catholic priest – work in a neighbourhood in New York City. Their dynamic and popular presence has a good influence on the local population. A third childhood friend, who has grown into a lovely young woman, turns up in their lives. A surprising and complicated love triangle develops among the three characters.

– Make a list of the moral dilemmas that this film brings to light.

– What are your reactions to the way in which the film's characters go about solving these problems?

Open the Bible

In Galilee, Jesus made choices that went against traditional ways of thinking and acting. He cared for the sick and for people who were on the fringes of society, he let children approach him, he spoke to women (this was frowned upon), and ate with sinners (even worse!). His choices sprang from his profound belief that human life is worth more than all the gold in the world. People are more important than laws, rules, profit, money or anything else. This fundamental belief gives meaning to his words and actions. Day after day, he upset preconceived ideas and values, and angered many of the local authorities. In a way, he was using his own life to build his cross. But he gave his life freely:

> "No one takes my life from me, but I lay it down of my own accord." (John 10:18)

- How do the choices Jesus had to make inspire you in your life?

Suggestions for Group Sharing

a) After a time of welcome and reflection, share your opinions on the three points of reference – freedom, conscience and responsibility – described earlier in this Path.

- How do you exercise your personal freedom when faced with pressure from society or your peers?

- How do you give your conscience the chance to be heard?

- What responsibilities are you facing in your life right now?

b) Do one of the Suggested Activities in this Path. If you wish, you can do the activity first individually, and then as a group.

c) Share your reactions to the homily Pope John Paul II gave in Israel on March 24, 2000 (see Appendix F).

d) End with the prayer for WYD 2002 (page 17).

e) Choose a path, date, time and place for your next meeting.

APPENDIX E

Blessed Gianna Beretta Molla (Italy, 1922–1962)

Gianna Beretta Molla was born in Magenta (Milan), Italy, on October 4, 1922, the 10th of 13 children. After earning degrees in medicine and surgery from the University of Pavia in 1949, she opened a medical clinic in Mesero (near Magenta) in 1950. She specialized in pediatrics at the University of Milan in 1952 and thereafter gave special attention to mothers, babies, the elderly and the poor. While working in the field of medicine – which she considered a "mission" and practised as such – she increased her generous service to Catholic Action, especially among the very young. She became engaged to Pietro Molla and they were married on September 24, 1955, in St. Martin's Basilica in Magenta. In November 1956, to her great joy, she became the mother of Pierluigi; in December 1957, of Mariolina; in July 1959, of Laura. With simplicity and great balance she met the demands of being a mother, wife and doctor and maintained her passion for life.

In September 1961, towards the end of the second month of pregnancy with her fourth child, Gianna had to make a heroic decision. Physicians diagnosed a serious fibroma in the uterus that required surgery. The surgeon suggested that Gianna undergo an abortion in order to save her own life. A few days before the child was due, she was ready to give her life in order to save that of her child: "If you must decide between me and the child, do not hesitate: choose the child – I insist on it. Save the baby." On the morning of April 21, 1962, Gianna Emanuela was born.

Despite all efforts and treatments to save both of them, on the morning of April 28, amid unspeakable pain and after repeated exclamations of "Jesus, I love you. Jesus, I love you," the mother died. She was 39 years old. Her husband, Pietro, described Gianna's life as "an act and a perennial action of faith and charity; it was a non-stop search for the will of God for every decision and for every task, with prayer and meditation, Holy Mass and the Eucharist."

On April 24, 1994, Pope John Paul II beatified Gianna Beretta Molla, mother of a family, in St. Peter's Square in Rome. The Pope said that her witness was a "hymn to life." Gianna continues to remind the Church and the world of the need for a consistent ethic of life, from the earliest moments to the final moments.

Virtuous people know what to do because of their informed conscience. This means that the person is living a morally good life and her decisions flow from a developed instinct for making truly human decisions. This type of person no longer does good out of a sense of obligation, but rather looks for opportunities to do good. Gianna Molla's action was heroic. The Pope, in the beatification ceremony, said that such an action was possible only after a lifetime of preparation. We are being called to heroism by our choice of life. By our Baptism, we are called to live Gospel values fully and to have an essential commitment to the Christ of the poor. Most of us are not ready for heroic action; our lives have not readied us for it. But we can and must take the next step in preparation for surrender of self. Let us ask Blessed Gianna to give us the courage to take the next step.

APPENDIX F

The Sermon on the Mount (Matthew 5:1-12)

When Jesus saw the crowds he went up the mountain; and after he sat down, his disciples came to him. Then he began to speak, and taught them, saying:

"Blessed are the poor in spirit, for theirs is the kingdom of heaven.

Blessed are those who mourn, for they will be comforted.

Blessed are the meek, for they will inherit the earth.

Blessed are those who hunger and thirst for righteousness, for they will be filled.

Blessed are the merciful, for they will receive mercy.

Blessed are the pure in heart, for they will see God.

Blessed are the peacemakers. For they will be called children of God.

Blessed are those who are persecuted for righteousness' sake, for theirs is the kingdom of heaven.

Blessed are you when people revile you and persecute you and utter all kinds of evil against you falsely on my account.

Rejoice and be glad, for your reward is great in heaven, for in the same way they persecuted the prophets who were before you."

Living the Beatitudes that Christ proclaimed in the Sermon on the Mount

Excerpts from the homily John Paul II preached on the Mount of the Beatitudes in Galilee on March 24, 2000. More than 100,000 were in attendance, most of them young people.

(...) How many generations before us have been deeply moved by the Sermon on the Mount! How many young people down the centuries have gathered around Jesus to learn the words of eternal life, as you are gathered here today! How many young hearts have been inspired by the power of his personality and the compelling truth of his message! It is wonderful that you are here!
(...)
The first to hear the Beatitudes of Jesus bore in their hearts the memory of another mountain – Mount Sinai. Just a month ago, I had the grace of going there, where God spoke to Moses and gave the Law, "written with the finger of God" (*Ex* 31:18) on the tablets of stone. These two mountains – Sinai and the Mount of the Beatitudes – offer us the roadmap of our Christian life and a summary of our responsibilities to God and neighbour. The Law and the Beatitudes together mark the path of the following of Christ and the royal road to spiritual maturity and freedom.

The Ten Commandments of Sinai may seem negative: "You will have no false gods before me; ... do not kill; do not commit adultery; do not steal; do not bear false witness..." (*Ex* 20:3, 13-16). But in fact they are supremely positive. Moving beyond the evil they name, they point the way to *the law of love* which is the first and greatest of the commandments: "You will love the Lord your God with all your heart, all your soul and all your mind. . . You will love your neighbour as yourself" (*Mt* 22:37, 39). Jesus himself says that he came not to abolish but to fulfil the Law (cf. *Mt* 5:17). His message is new but it does not destroy what went before; it leads what went before to its fullest potential. Jesus teaches that the way of love brings the Law to fulfilment (cf. *Gal* 5:14). And he taught this enormously important truth on this hill here in Galilee.

"Blessed are you!", he says "all you who are poor in spirit, gentle and merciful, you who mourn, who care for what is right, who are pure in heart, who make peace, you who are persecuted! Blessed are you!" But the words of Jesus may seem strange. It is strange that Jesus exalts those whom the world generally regards as weak. He says to them, "Blessed are you who seem to be losers, because you are the true winners: the kingdom of heaven is yours!" Spoken by him who is "gentle and humble in heart" (*Mt* 11:29), these words present a challenge which demands a deep and abiding *metanoia* of the spirit, a great change of heart.

You young people will understand why this change of heart is necessary! Because you are aware of another voice within you and all around you, a contradictory voice. It is a voice which says, "Blessed are the proud and violent, those who prosper at any cost, who are unscrupulous, pitiless, devious, who make war not peace, and persecute those who stand in their way". And this voice seems to make sense in a world where the violent often triumph and the devious seem to succeed. "Yes", says the voice of evil, "they are the ones who win. Happy are they!"

Jesus offers a very different message. Not far from this very place Jesus called his first disciples, as he calls you now. His call has always demanded a choice between the two voices competing for your hearts even now on this hill, the choice between good and evil, between life and death. Which voice will the young people of the twenty-first century choose to follow? To put your faith in Jesus means choosing to believe what he says, no matter how strange it may seem, and choosing to reject the claims of evil, no matter how sensible or attractive they may seem.

In the end, Jesus does not merely speak the Beatitudes. He lives the Beatitudes. He is the Beatitudes. Looking at him you will see what it means to be poor in spirit, gentle and merciful, to mourn, to care for what is right, to be pure in heart, to make peace, to be persecuted. This is why he has the right to say, "Come, follow *me*!" He does not say simply, "Do what I say". He says, "Come, follow *me*!"

You hear his voice on this hill, and you believe what he says. But like the first disciples at the Sea of Galilee, you must leave your boats and nets behind, and that is never easy – especially when you face an uncertain future and are tempted to lose faith in your Christian heritage. To be good Christians may seem beyond your strength in today's world. But Jesus does not stand by and leave you alone to face the challenge. He is always with you to transform your weakness into strength. Trust him when he says: "My grace is enough for you, for my power is made perfect in weakness" (*2 Cor* 12:9)!

The disciples spent time with the Lord. They came to know and love him deeply. They discovered the meaning of what the Apostle Peter once said to Jesus: "Lord, to whom shall we go? You have the words of eternal life" (*Jn* 6:68). They discovered that the words of eternal life are the words of Sinai and the words of the Beatitudes. And this is the message which they spread everywhere. (...)

path 5

2000 YEARS YOUNG

The Church:
an ever-changing community

An invitation from John Paul II

> Your generation is being challenged in a special way to keep
> safe the deposit of faith (cf. *2 Th* 2:15; *1 Tim* 6:20; *2 Tim* 1:14).
> Discover your Christian roots, learn about the Church's history,
> deepen your knowledge of the spiritual heritage which has
> been passed on to you, follow in the footsteps of the witnesses
> and teachers who have gone before you!
> (…)
>
> Yes, now is the time for mission! In your Dioceses and parishes,
> in your movements, associations and communities, Christ is
> calling you. The Church welcomes you and wishes to be your
> home and your school of communion and prayer.
>
> *(Message of the Holy Father for WYD 2002)*

A beer commercial highlights the company's longevity with the phrase
"Young since 1903." What would you say about a Church that has
been young for 2000 years – from John the Apostle in the year 30 to
the hundreds of thousands of young people gathering in Toronto in
2002? Not to mention people like Francis of Assisi in the 13th century,
Therese of Lisieux in the 19th century and Karol Wotjyla (who would
become Pope John Paul II) in 1940s Poland. "The spirit blows where
it will." We might add that it keeps blowing fresh air!

The young and the not-so-young walk in Christ's footsteps. They carry
out projects and take action. In doing so, they become disciples and
gather strength from a Church that provides them with resources and
community. They are witnesses of the kingdom to others through
prayer and solidarity, among other things.

- Do you consider yourself to be a member of the Church?

- If not, why?

- If you do, what is your gift to the Christian community as a
  member of the Church?

The Church as a community: Yesterday and today

One of the stories in the New Testament takes place during Pentecost. It was a very special day: a celebration of the harvest and of the Covenant between God and his people. This is the day the Spirit, whom Jesus had promised to send, descended on the gathered apostles and disciples. Filled with new-found courage, Peter spoke to the Jews who had come from all over to celebrate Pentecost. He bore witness to the death and resurrection of Jesus. Everyone present was able to understand him in their native language! Nothing could stop the disciples from sharing the Good News that day, not even threats from the authorities. They were bound together by the same faith, the same community: the Church.

Little by little, the group of Christians grew. The first communities developed guidelines that would allow them to carry out their mission: together they prayed, went to the Temple, listened to the teachings and testimonies of the apostles, broke bread and shared their worldly goods (Acts 2:42). The Eucharist, in memory of Jesus' death and resurrection, united them and created community among them.

The young adults who attended WYD 2000 in Rome lived a similar experience of community. Many bore witness. Let us listen to what two of them had to say:

"Our participation in WYD 2000 allowed us to expand our vision of the Church. We no longer see the Church as just a place to pray, but as a sharing, helping, generous community willing to reach out to the world.

"Our vision of the Church has changed a lot! We discovered a worldwide community of faith in Jesus Christ. The presence of so many young people at WYD 2000 showed us that the Church is alive and well, contrary to what many people think. Furthermore, young adults dare to affirm their faith out loud! We dream of an even more human Church, one that is even more accessible and closer to people's lives. We also dream of a Church that is more open to new realities. We dream of a Church that trusts youth, and a Church that many will come back to freely. Finally, we dream of a Church that is open to all religions proclaiming that every human being has the potential to become better."

—*G.A. and P.C.*

• Compare your vision of the Church to the one described above. What are the similarities? What are the differences?

A mission

The first disciples had a huge mission: to bring out the best in each man and woman. To do this, they tried to live as Jesus taught them:

• to prefer service over glory (Mark 9:35);

• to give priority to the poorest among them (Matthew 10:17 and following);

• to gather in prayer (Matthew 10:6);

• to not fear persecution (Matthew 18:19);

• to forgive each other (Matthew 18:23).

This was and is the Church's mission! Then, as now, these values went against the mainstream, which was more concerned with prestige, social status and power struggles.

Today's disciples follow the very same Jesus, who died and rose again. Filled with the Spirit, they form the new "people of God," where everyone has a unique role to play. They want to free humanity from distress and to bring hope. They follow the path of believers who, throughout the ages, worked for the same goals: Francis of Assisi, Claire of Assisi, Benedict, Vincent de Paul, John Bosco, Marguerite Bourgeoys, Marguerite d'Youville, Jeanne Mance, and many, many more.

• Can you think of a pressing need in your area that the local Christian community could meet?

• Would you be willing to participate in such an activity?

The Church calls all believers to open their eyes to the world, to fight against everything that is dehumanizing and against everything that destroys human dignity.

Christ is present in this world that he loves through his body, the Church.

"Just as the body is one and has many members, and all the members of the body, though many, are one body, so it is with Christ. For in the one Spirit we were all baptized into one body." (1 Corinthians 12:12-13) Through his body, the Church, Christ continues to proclaim the Kingdom, care for the sick and feed the hungry.

One Spirit

As John Paul II reminds us in his apostolic letter on the new millennium, the Church can only carry out its mission if believers unite and stay in "communion" with one another:

This makes us able to share [our brothers' and sisters'] joys and sufferings, to sense their desires and attend to their needs, to offer them deep and genuine friendship. A spirituality of communion implies also the ability to see what is positive in others, to welcome it and prize it as a gift from God: not only as a gift for the brother or sister who has received it directly, but also as a 'gift for me.' A spirituality of communion means, finally, to know how to 'make room' for our brothers and sisters, bearing 'each other's burdens' (*Gal* 6:2) and resisting the selfish temptations which constantly beset us and provoke competition, careerism, distrust and jealousy. Let us have no illusions: unless we follow this spiritual path, external structures of communion will serve very little purpose. (*Novo millenio ineunte*, no. 43)

Some participants in WYD 2000 tell us of the communion they experienced there:

"There were so many different cultures and faces in Rome… but we were all doing the same thing and were there for the same reason: God. WYD gave me a taste of what heaven must be like. Heaven will be like a melody made up of voices from different languages all singing the same song. Each person will sing their own part in their own way, but it will make one beautiful song."

—N.T.

"I felt like we had a direct line to God, all this goodness. I really felt connected to that. We really felt like the Pope was comfortable with young people and that he wants us to feel comfortable in the Church."
—C.S.

"I am from Northern Canada and WYD 2000 was my first time abroad. It was incredible to be in St. Peter's Square… This Church, with all the gifts and talents people have given throughout the years… The whole experience confirmed for me again that Christ is alive! I felt transformed and I wanted to begin living out my faith as soon as I got home!"

—J.B.

- What will it take for you to experience "communion" during WYD 2002?
- How is "communion" expressed in your local community?

Constant adjustments

Over the centuries, the Church has certainly had to make changes and deal with tensions and even conflicts. In the earliest Christian communities, the mixing of different cultures led to dissension: Christians of Jewish origin lived side by side with Christians of Greek origin, and crises loomed. For example, in order to discuss whether non-Jews needed to be circumcised, Peter called the first council, in Jerusalem. This gives an idea of how important this question was to the early Church. They decided that circumcision was not obligatory.

Since then, other councils have been called to discuss current issues and respond to them in the best way possible for that time. The last council met from 1962 to 1965 in Rome at the invitation of Pope John XXIII. It was called "Vatican II" because it was the second council held in the Vatican. Vatican II brought about important changes in the Church.

Roles and responsibilities

As Jesus taught us (Matthew 20:25), authority does not grant superiority. Authority is a way to serve others.

In the early Church

The growing number of disciples forced the twelve apostles to get organized in order to spread the Good News more efficiently. There were many different roles, as there are today, even if some of the names have fallen out of use: elders (1 Timothy 4:14), prophets (1 Corinthians 14:3), catechists (Acts 2:42), doctors (1 Corinthians 12:27), bishops (1 Timothy 3:1-5), and deacons (1 Timothy 3:8-12).

It is also worth noting that women had an important place in the early Church, given the mentality of the time: Phoebe was a deaconess (Romans 16:1-12); Prisca collaborated with Paul (Romans 16:3); Mary devoted herself to prayer and to the service of the Word (Romans 6:6); Junias was referred to as an apostle by Paul (Romans 16:7).

In the Church today

The Church today, like the early Church, is defined by diversity and unity, in one faith.

Eastern churches provide us with one of the greatest illustrations of "diversity in unity." (See "The Eastern Catholic Churches," Appendix G, for further details.)

In order for the Church to work as a cohesive unit, it has been necessary to establish structures and functions over the centuries.

salt and light

The Pope is the most visible function in the Church. He is responsible for the "authenticity of the faith," or ensuring that the Church conforms with the testimonies of the earliest Christian communities and Jesus' message. One day Jesus said to Peter (the first pope):

> *"And I tell you, you are Peter, and on this rock I will build my church, and the gates of Hades will not prevail against it. I will give you the keys of the kingdom of heaven, and whatever you bind on earth will be bound in heaven, and whatever you loose on earth will be loosed in heaven."* (Matthew 16:18-19)

John Paul II is heir to this task, serving the communion between local churches.

- How can you serve the Church and the world? What vocation will you choose for this service? (Lay person, religious sister or brother, deacon, priest...)

- Consider the origins of the Church. What aspects of the early Church can help the Church today to fulfill its mission?

Suggested Activities

- Write a letter describing your vision of the Church to your bishop or to another person who has responsibilities in your local Church. What, in your opinion, are some new ways in which the Church can reach out to young people?

- Invite people from your area to a forum on the role of the Church in today's world: its relevance, the urgent needs it must meet, and the different responsibilities its members – the young and adults of all ages – must take on.

- Learn more about the Eastern rite churches (see Appendix G) and compare their rites to those of the Roman Church.

- Come up with an innovative idea for the members of your local Christian community that will make your community more "interesting" for you and other people you know, like the first Christians did (see "Open the Bible," below).

Open the Bible

The following verse, from the New Testament's Acts of the Apostles, sums up the life and mission of the Church:

> *"They devoted themselves to the apostles' teaching and fellowship, to the breaking of bread and the prayers."* (Acts 2:42)

- Referring to this quote, identify some activities that already exist in your local Christian community, or activities that can be put into place to

– encourage people in their spiritual life (prayer),

– proclaim the Gospel (the apostles' teaching),

– make the Eucharist meaningful (breaking bread),

– show solidarity with the poor (fellowship).

Suggestions for Group Sharing

a) After a time of welcome and reflection, invite each person to read individually the passages from "A mission" (page 74) and/or "One Spirit" (page 75). Then ask for a volunteer to tell of an experience of community that he or she has had.

b) Share your opinions about this person's experience and ask those who wish to do so to describe the Church of their dreams:

- discuss roles and responsibilities within the Church,
- discuss the challenges it faces,
- discern what you would like to do.

c) Do one of the Suggested Activities in this Path or another activity you have chosen.

d) Close with the prayer for WYD 2002 (page 17).

e) Choose the path, date, time and place for your next meeting.

APPENDIX G

The Eastern Catholic Churches

During its history, the Catholic Church has not always followed one model. Although the faith and the ideals of Christian life are the same always and everywhere, we find a variety of models in the Church. This vision of unity in diversity is clearly evident in the Eastern Catholic Churches. In his apostolic letter *Orientale Lumen* [The Light of the East], Pope John Paul II explains:

> From the beginning, the Christian East has proved to contain a wealth of forms capable of assuming the characteristic features of each individual culture, with supreme respect for each particular community. (no. 5)

Ever since Jesus instructed the apostles to go out into the world and make disciples of all the nations, the early Christian Church grew and expanded into each region of the Roman Empire and beyond. By the fourth century, a number of distinct Christian communities had already formed according to different traditions, cultures, customs, languages, art, architecture and music. These churches, both within the Roman Empire and outside it, are now commonly called the Eastern Catholic churches. Today, there are 21 Eastern Catholic churches, each one independent from the others. Each of these churches grew out of one of the four original Eastern traditions or rites: that of Alexandria, Antioch, Armenia and Byzantium. These churches, each in its own way and according to its own history, often found themselves in the same geographical areas as each other, due to the immigration and migration of the faithful throughout the world.

With the exception of the Maronite Church and the Italo-Albanian Church, all the Eastern Catholic churches were, at one time or another in their history, out of communion with Rome because of controversies related to doctrine or to matters of faith. Gradually, some groups and sometimes even entire churches re-established communion with Rome while keeping their own traditions. Nevertheless, many groups and Eastern (Orthodox) churches continued to exist apart from the

Universal (Catholic) Church. This fact explains why most Eastern Catholic Churches have an orthodox faction. For example, there is a Coptic Orthodox Church, a Ukrainian Orthodox Church, a Russian Orthodox Church, and so on. The Eastern Catholic Churches and the Orthodox Churches often co-exist in the same city, village or rural area. They share identical liturgical traditions, customs, and cultures. What distinguishes them, and what divides them, is the issue of communion with Rome: the Eastern Catholic churches are in communion with Rome, while the Orthodox churches are independent of and separate from Rome.

The faith of each of the Eastern churches has always been deeply rooted in and lived through the liturgy, which is where the confession of faith, praise and witness take place. In other words, if you wish to know more about the Eastern Catholic churches, take part in one of their liturgies. You will find many references to the Trinitarian God presented as a divine and unfathomable mystery that is beyond human knowledge and understanding. This explains why, for example, the eucharistic bread and wine are covered by a veil even when presented to the community, and why adoration of the eucharist is not a custom in the Eastern churches.

Although we are mindful that we are unable to know and understand the life and mystery of God, we are still invited to "become participants of the divine nature" (2 Peter 1:4). This invitation is made possible by the life, death and resurrection of Jesus Christ. Created in the image of God, we have the ability and the potential, by means of our free response, to become like God. This explains why the text and the plan of many Eastern Catholic liturgies try to give a foretaste of full communion between heaven and earth, of our full communion with God. The priest guides the community in this journey towards heaven, which explains why he turns his back to the community so often during the Eastern rite liturgical celebrations. During a eucharistic celebration you will notice a lot of movement and processions. Incense is often used. The walls and the entrance to the sanctuary, particularly in Byzantine Catholic and Coptic churches, are covered with icons (a word that means "image" in Greek). The icons illustrate the public teaching of the Church and the presence of God in an effort to open the windows on heaven.

For Eastern Catholics, one's relationship with Christ becomes the "door" by which communion with God becomes possible. Eastern Churches often use the theme of light to show the "transformative" nature of our life in Christ. Life in Christ calls people to let themselves be transformed by means of a life of prayer and participation in the holy mysteries (sacraments). Mary, the Mother of God, the Theotokos (God-bearer), becomes a model for all Christians. She is often commemorated in Eastern rite liturgical celebrations because of her role in the history of redemption, especially her willingness to say yes to God. The Eastern churches also place great importance on the communion of saints in honour of their efforts to become "participants" in the divine nature.

In spite of these common approaches, different liturgical traditions, music and customs exist among the Eastern churches. One simple but significant example is the many different names for the eucharistic liturgy. The Byzantine churches speak of the "Divine Liturgy"; the Maronite Church refers to "The divine service of the Holy Mysteries"; other Eastern churches refer to "The Offertory"; others, "Consecration"; still others, "the Mass." While some Eastern churches (such as Coptics, Melkites, Ukrainians, and Syrians) use leavened bread for their eucharistic celebrations, some (such as Armenians, Maronites, and Chaldeans) use unleavened bread. Most of the Eastern churches have developed their own melodic systems for music, which vary according to the liturgical season.

Much more could be said about Eastern Catholic churches, but one fact remains: these churches are important to the life of the whole Catholic Church. With the Western churches, the Eastern churches are the inheritors of the Gospel message, and are called to proclaim this message to the whole world.

An Eastern rite Catholic is declared a saint

P. Zenovij Kovalyk, C.Ss.R

Blessed Zenovij (Zenon) Kovalyk, Ukrainian (Eastern) Catholic, Redemptorist priest (1903–1941)

Father Zenovij was an eloquent preacher who spoke his mind. During the Second World War, he preached openly against the atheistic communist regime. In spite of warnings from his friends and fellow priests that he was in danger, Father Zenovij kept speaking out, saying, "I will die joyfully if that is the will of God, but I will never go against my conscience." On December 20, 1939, he was arrested while preaching a sermon on the Immaculate Conception of Mary, Mother of God. Imprisoned at Lviv, he underwent 28 interrogations, which included torture. He kept preaching in prison, and prayed with the prisoners. In 1941, the Soviets, recalling his sermons on the crucified Christ, nailed him to a prison wall rather than shooting him, as they did with other prisoners. He died a martyr for his faith at age 37. He was beatified in June 2001 by Pope John Paul II during his visit to Ukraine.

GIVE ME A SIGN!

Prayer, sacraments and celebration

An invitation from John Paul II

> Study the Word of God and let it enlighten your minds and hearts. Draw strength from the sacramental grace of Reconciliation and the Eucharist. Visit the Lord in that "heart to heart" contact that is Eucharistic Adoration. Day after day, you will receive new energy to help you to bring comfort to the suffering and peace to the world.
>
> *(Message of the Holy Father for WYD 2002)*

Most of the young people who participated in WYD 2000 in Rome and who share the story of their journey speak of the importance of prayer in their lives. Many express their joy in participating in the sacraments. Almost all attach particular importance to celebrating their faith in God, of "living it up" with God. Here is what one young woman says:

> "This pilgrimage has also been for me an experience of prayer. Group prayer... personal prayer, too, where I give my life to the Lord... but also, above all, where I let Jesus speak to me. (...) During the pilgrimage, my life was really prayer and I want that to continue. (...) I feel strengthened in my faith and especially in my way of life."
>
> —G.R.

If you hear my voice...

When everything seems to be going wrong, we sometimes say, "Where is God?" or "If there is a God who can hear me..." Other people, especially older people, might say, "What have I done to God to make this happen?" This is already a prayer, but we must admit that, at times like these, trust is not ruling our lives.

And yet, in the New Testament, we read these amazing words:

> *Listen! I am standing at the door, knocking; if you hear my voice and open the door, I will come in to you and eat with you, and you with me.* (Revelation 3:20)

Strange, isn't it? When we say, "If there is a God who can hear me…" do we know that God is also trying to be heard?

"Study the Word of God and let it enlighten your minds and hearts," says John Paul II.

"I let Jesus speak to me," says the young woman who went on pilgrimage to WYD 2000.

As in all relationships, prayer is not a one-way street!

• Do you ever pray? How do you pray?

An unexpected guest

The first step towards dialogue is to open your heart, to let the Word of God enter and live in your house. But be careful… the guest is unpredictable! He might come in through silence and meditation, of course, but also through the hubbub of studying, working, sports and recreation. Through a friend who has upset your plans. Through the poor person who asks for your time or money. Through the people in a developing country who depend on the solidarity of their brothers and sisters across the world. Through conversations with your family or your co-workers, or through political discussions. In the safe place of your room or in a public place.

Does all this have something to do with prayer? Yes, all this and more. "Day after day, you will receive new energy to help you to bring comfort to the suffering and peace to the world," says Pope John Paul II.

When Jesus wanted to pray, he went into the desert, but he didn't do this every day. Some Christian communities, when they want to pray, go to church, but their prayer is not confined to the church. Christian prayer is not just words; it has arms and hands, too.

The prayer of Jesus

And after he had dismissed the crowds, he went up the mountain by himself to pray. When evening came, he was there alone...
(Matthew 14:23)

Like all Jews, Jesus knew well the prayers of Israel. The big book of prayers for the Jewish people is the book of Psalms found in the Bible. The book of Psalms contains prayers of adoration, praise, demands and – why not? – discouragement. Jesus no doubt recited the Psalms, alone or with his disciples. His prayer was life and his life was prayer. It was like a kind of breathing.

Here is how Jesus gave prayer a new dimension, by giving God the name *Abba* (Father). What a scandal this was for the Jews around him: Jesus prayed to God as a son speaks to his father, and taught us to pray that way, too.

"Pray then in this way:

Our Father in heaven,

hallowed be your name.

Your kingdom come.

Your will be done,

on earth as it is in heaven.

Give us this day our daily bread.

And forgive us our debts,

as we also have forgiven our debtors.

And do not bring us to the time of trial,

but rescue us from the evil one."

(Matthew 6:9-13)

Calling God "Father": What do you think?

Calling God "Father" makes us sons and daughters, but also brothers and sisters. Even in the silence of the human heart, Christian prayer is never individual in the sense of being detached from other people. Christian prayer is fundamentally connected to the community. Thus, by adopting the prayer Jesus taught, we pray as a Church, as a community.

The prayer of the Church

For Jesus to talk to God as if God was his father seemed bold. But Jesus didn't stop there. He also said: *"The Father and I are one"* (John 10:30). After that, the disciples began to pray to Jesus, as they prayed to the Father. The apostle Thomas said to Jesus: *"My Lord and my God!"* (John 20:28).

After the resurrection of Jesus, the "first Church" discovered the presence of the Holy Spirit, as Jesus had promised: *"the Advocate, the Holy Spirit, whom the Father will send in my name"* (John 14:26). After the Jewish feast of Pentecost, the apostles and Mary, the mother of Jesus, received the gift of the Holy Spirit, who gave new breath to their lives and to their prayer:

> *When they had prayed, the place in which they were gathered together was shaken; and they were all filled with the Holy Spirit and spoke the word of God with boldness.* (Acts 4:31)

From its earliest days, the Church knew God as Father, Son and Spirit. The apostle Paul witnessed to this in his letters to the Christian communities:

> *And because you are children, God has sent the Spirit of his Son into our hearts, crying, "Abba! Father!"* (Galatians 4:6)

This faith has never ceased to express itself in the prayer of the Church:

> Glory to the Father, and to the Son, and to the Holy Spirit,
> As it was in the beginning, is now, and ever shall be.

God is love. When God gives of himself, it is to be shared. God is not alone in God's "kingdom." On the cross, Jesus said to the thief who asked Jesus to remember him, *"Today you will be with me in Paradise"* (Luke 23:43).

Those who open the door of their hearts to God find themselves close to God. These may be the saints who are recognized by the Church, but also others, such as our family members and friends who have died but who during their lives had let themselves be touched by the love of God.

Close to God is Mary, the mother of Jesus, of course. We can no longer count the number of feasts of Mary, titles given to Mary, and prayers to Mary. In the faith of the Church there is the conviction that Mary "intercedes" for us with God, as the Church asks her to do every day in this simple prayer:

> Hail Mary, full of grace,
>
> the Lord is with you.
>
> Blessed are you among women
>
> And blessed is the fruit of your womb, Jesus.
>
> Holy Mary, Mother of God,
>
> Pray for us sinners,
>
> Now and at the hour of our death.

One of the titles given to Mary is "Our Lady of Guadalupe."

Listen to John Paul II as he talks about the importance of Mary:

How can we fail to emphasize the role which belongs to the Virgin Mary in relation to the pilgrim Church in America journeying towards its encounter with the Lord?
(...)
Throughout the continent, from the time of the first evangelization, the presence of the Mother of God has been strongly felt, thanks to the efforts of the missionaries. In their preaching, "the Gospel was proclaimed by presenting the Virgin Mary as its highest realization. From the beginning – invoked as Our Lady of Guadalupe – Mary, by her motherly and merciful figure, was a great sign of the closeness of the Father and of Jesus Christ, with whom she invites us to enter into communion".

The appearance of Mary to the native Juan Diego on the hill of Tepeyac in 1531 had a decisive effect on evangelization. Its influence greatly overflows the boundaries of Mexico, spreading to the whole Continent. America, which historically has been, and still is, a melting-pot of peoples, has recognized in the *mestiza* face of the Virgin of Tepeyac, "in Blessed Mary of Guadalupe, an impressive example of a perfectly inculturated evangelization". Consequently, not only in Central and South America, but in North America as well, the Virgin of Guadalupe is venerated as Queen of all America.
(...)
In view of this, I welcome with joy the proposal of the Synod Fathers that the feast of Our Lady of Guadalupe, Mother and Evangelizer of America, be celebrated throughout the continent on December 12.

(John Paul II, Post-synodal Exhortation *Ecclesia in America* [The Church in America], 1999, no. 11)

salt and light

The *Our Father...* the *Glory to the Father, to the Son and to the Holy Spirit...* the *Hail Mary...* these three prayers have spread everywhere throughout the Catholic Church. Even the rosary has these prayers as its foundation. As we begin the rosary with the *Sign of the Cross* and the *Creed,* we place it within a summary of the faith of the Church:

> I believe in God, the Father almighty, creator of heaven and earth.

> I believe in Jesus Christ, his only Son, our Lord. He was conceived by the power of the Holy Spirit and born of the Virgin Mary. He suffered under Pontius Pilate, was crucified, died, and was buried. He descended to the dead. On the third day he rose again. He ascended into heaven, and is seated at the right hand of the Father. He will come again to judge the living and the dead.

> I believe in the Holy Spirit, the holy catholic Church, the communion of saints, the forgiveness of sins, the resurrection of the body, and the life everlasting. Amen.

The sacraments: Signs of life

Remember: God gives us a sign by knocking on the door. The greatest sign of God's love is his Son, Jesus, whom he sent to us. Jesus is the actual presence of God in the life of the world. The Church is called to become in its turn the sign of the presence of Christ among us, as Christ himself asked:

> *Go therefore and make disciples of all nations, baptizing them in the name of the Father and of the Son and of the Holy Spirit, and teaching them to obey everything that I have commanded you. And remember, I am with you always, to the end of time.* (Matthew 28:19-20)

Have you ever noticed that a true friend is never really absent? That friend remains present in some way all the time. He or she may call, write or e-mail just to give a "sign of life." The sacraments are something like that – we exchange signs of life with Jesus.

To show our love to someone, we might decide to give flowers. Flowers become a sign of love: they point towards something else, towards what they are expressing. The sacraments, which are the signs of the presence of Jesus in Christian life, point towards forgiveness, communion, promise, trust, charity and justice.

A young woman who was at WYD 2000 wants to be reconciled with God. Listen to how she tells the story of what happened to her in Rome:

> "After a break in a park near the basilica, Allan, 'our' priest, offered to welcome us for the sacrament of reconciliation. It was under a palm tree, away from the crowd, that the Lord welcomed me. At that moment, I felt as if I didn't have to go towards God, to look for God. Instead, it was God who was coming towards me, just when I didn't expect it."
>
> —J.M.

- Have you ever exchanged "signs of life" with Jesus? What were they?

The seven sacraments: The colours of life

- The birth of a child is an intense time that summons the life force of the child and recalls our hopes and our fears. In the case of baptism of a young person or an adult, we can talk about their own hopes and fears. **Baptism** celebrates the loving presence of God.

- Self-affirmation is difficult work that calls to our **daring** and connects us to our **doubts**. **Confirmation** celebrates the active presence of the Spirit.

- Friendship and fraternity call to our desire to **share** and make us question our tendencies to **turn in** on ourselves. The **Eucharist** celebrates Jesus, who gives himself and invites us into communion with him.

- Forgiveness calls to our **openness** to others and asks us to challenge our **limits**. The sacrament of **Reconciliation** celebrates the mercy of God, who repairs the links that we have broken.

- Love calls to our **dreams** of love and reconnects us when we find it **difficult** to love. The sacrament of **Marriage** celebrates the presence of God at the heart of the love between spouses.

- Consecrated life calls to our **gift of self** and gets us in touch with our **difficulty** in giving of ourselves to others. The sacrament of **Orders** celebrates God's call to put ourselves at the service of the Church alone.

- Illness is an intense moment that calls us to **courage** and puts us in touch with our **fear**. The sacrament of **Anointing of the Sick** celebrates the presence of Jesus at the heart of our suffering.

(Office de catéchèse du Québec [Catechetical Office of Quebec], *Rites et célébrations* [Rites and celebrations], *Le cœur sur la main* [Heart in Hand] Collection. Montreal/Ottawa: Fides, Médiaspaul, Novalis, page 24.)

The celebration: Place of forgiveness, of communion and of the feast

We have all celebrated love and friendship. We have all marked the important moments or passages in our lives.

Every day, we live through passages: from conflict to reconciliation, from solitude to relationship, from illness to healing, from joy to sadness and then from sadness to joy. Our life journey is marked by important passages: birth, childhood and adolescence, entry into the workforce, major decisions of all kinds. Often we feel the need to highlight these moments, to deepen our sense of the importance of the moment or to share them with others:

- Couples paint their names on a rock at the side of the road.
- People or groups keep a journal where they can record their thoughts.
- Families gather to mourn the loss of a loved one.
- People organize parties to celebrate reunions.

At church, through the liturgical and sacramental celebration, we place our passages under the sign of the Passover, the greatest passage, the passage from death to life! We celebrate the resurrection of Jesus in our joy as in our pain, in our love and our reasons for living, in our personal and community obligations.

Yet to understand a sign, one must be "initiated" – one must know to what the sign points. If I don't know that a white flag means a call for truce, I might shoot someone who is seeking peace! In the same way, without Christian initiation, people risk seeing liturgical celebrations and the sacraments simply as cultural or social actions, without being open to the presence of God. The sacraments express faith but also presume that faith exists, in the same way that giving a bouquet of flowers to a loved one presumes the affection that is expressed by this gesture. The more alive faith is, the more the sacraments find their place in a person's life.

- Which bible passages shed light on the meaning of the sacraments?

salt and light

Suggested Activities

- Talk to someone who is preparing to celebrate one of the sacraments for the first time (such as parents who are presenting their child for Baptism; a young person who is preparing for First Communion or Confirmation; or a couple planning to marry) about what the sacrament means to them.

- Make a note of any questions about prayer and the rites of the Church that you have and ask to meet with someone who can help guide you, such as a priest or a pastoral minister.

Open the Bible

Rather than just getting a brief glimpse of the Word of God, let us take the time to "study the Word of God," as John Paul II invites us. Let the Word of God "enlighten your minds and hearts," and draw strength from the sacramental grace of Reconciliation and the Eucharist.

In Appendix I, you will find two biblical passages to explore: the prodigal son and the road to Emmaus.

Suggestions for Group Sharing

Note: You can integrate this meeting with a eucharistic celebration, or prepare a celebration for your next meeting.

a) At the beginning of the session (or the celebration), place on a table several objects, including a bottle of oil, a baptismal candle, a wedding ring, a cross, a flower, a jar of water.

Ask participants to say what these objects represent for them. If people are reluctant to speak, ask them each to take one object and say what possible meanings that object could have. Then you can reflect on the symbol, what it represents, what it points to.

b) Read aloud a passage of your choice from Path 6. Invite participants to give their reaction to the passage. Invite those who wish to do so to talk about the place prayer has in their lives. Here are some suggestions for prompting discussion:

- When do you feel the need to pray?
- Describe one such situation. How did you live through this? What role did prayer play for you?

c) Together, do the activity on the disciples on the road to Emmaus (Appendix I), or prepare a celebration that integrates this passage.

d) Close with the prayer for WYD 2002 (page 17).

e) Choose the path, date, time and place for your next meeting (or for your celebration).

APPENDIX H

The prayer life of the saints

The saints – those great witnesses of the Gospel who often began and directed incredible works – were also men and women of prayer. Even in the midst of major responsibilities, rather than reducing the amount of time they gave to prayer, they would increase it.

For St. Teresa of Avila (16th century), "Prayer is talking to God as if to a friend who we know loves us." Madeleine Delbrel, an involved laywoman (20th century), talks about the central importance that prayer has in her day: "Praying is taking time away from doing 'useful' things in order to become even more useful." For Marie (Guyart) de l'Incarnation, one of the first religious to arrive in Quebec from France in the 16th century, Jesus says to us through prayer, "You will know me by loving me." "God gives us all we can hope for," said Saint John of the Cross about prayer.

Kateri Tekakwitha (1656–1680)

She was called "Tekakwitha" (one who moves forward by feeling the way) because her eyesight was weak; she had had smallpox as a child. She was baptized in 1676 with the name Catherine, or Kateri in Iroquois. Persecuted by her family for becoming a Christian, she lived at the St. Francis Xavier Christian mission on the south shore of the St. Lawrence River, at Kahnawake. Katerie loved to pray and go to Mass; with a friend, she hoped to found a religious community for native women. Instead, she died at age 24 as a result of illness. Those who knew her mourned her deeply. She was known as a model of deep faith and trust in "what pleases God," which was her motto. She was declared "venerable" by Pope Pius XII on January 3, 1943, and "blessed" by John Paul II on June 22, 1980.

APPENDIX I

Celebrating reconciliation:
A step towards freedom and healing

The biblical text we suggest is that of the merciful father and the prodigal son (Luke 15:11-32). Try to identify with the characters in the story to discover the blessings of reconciliation with God and to prepare for the sacrament of Reconciliation with a priest.

Welcome:

> *A man had two sons. The younger of them said to his father: "Father, give me the share of the property that will belong to me." So he divided his property between them. A few days later the younger son gathered all he had and travelled to a distant country, and there he squandered his property in dissolute living.... I will get up and go to my father, and I will say to him, "Father, I have sinned against heaven and before you; I am no longer worthy to be called your son; treat me like one of your hired hands." So he set off and went to his father.*

The sacrament of Reconciliation is not limited to our meeting with the priest. It begins at the moment when the desire and the need for reconciliation with God are born. When I look at my life in light of the Word of God, as Saint Paul said, I am aware that I do the things I do not want to do, and the good I want to do, I do not do. I feel the need to say this to the priest who welcomes me, to whom I speak as to a friend, as I tell him about how hard it is to make good triumph in my life.

The word, which heals and frees us:

> *But while he was still far off, his father saw him and was filled with compassion; he ran and put his arms around him and kissed him. Then the son said, "Father, I have sinned against heaven and before you; I am no longer worthy to be called your son."*

God comes to meet me in the sacrament of Reconciliation, and delights in forgiveness as much as I do. *"There is joy in the presence of the angels of God over one sinner who repents."* (Luke 15:10)

* I take the time to confess my sins. The priest can help me by asking me to do something or by giving me guidance. I finish with a prayer that shows my desire for conversion, such as the Jesus Prayer: "Lord Jesus Christ, son of the living God, have mercy on me, a sinner."

* The priest says the words of absolution: "God the Father, by the death and resurrection of his Son, has reconciled the world to himself and has sent the Holy Spirit among us for the forgiveness of sins. Through the ministry of the Church, may God grant you pardon and peace, and I absolve you from all your sins, in the name of the Father and of the Son and of the Holy Spirit."

Thanksgiving and sending forth to mission:

> *The father said to his slaves, "Quickly, bring out a robe – the best one – and put it on him; put a ring on his finger and sandals on his feet. And get the fatted calf and kill it, and let us eat and celebrate; for this son of mine was dead and is alive again; he was lost and is found! And they began to celebrate.*

* The priest sends me forth into the world to witness through my life each day to the joy of forgiveness. Through acts of peace and self-denial, I witness to the forgiveness I received.

The eucharistic celebration:
Source and summit of the sacramental life

The biblical text we suggest here is that of the disciples on the road to Emmaus (Luke 24:13-35). Let yourselves be guided by them; even better, put yourselves on the road with them. Play the role of the third disciple who has travelled in time to join their conversation.

Gathering and welcome:

> [On the third day after Jesus died] two of [the disciples] were going to a village called Emmaus, about seven miles from Jerusalem, and talking with each other about all these things that had happened. While they were talking and discussing, Jesus himself came near and went with them, but their eyes were kept from recognizing him.

Jesus had been put to death! The rabbi or teacher who had given them so much hope, the "liberator of Israel," had been crucified with thieves! The collapse of their hopes, and their disappointment, could be seen in their eyes. Then a stranger joined them and asked them what they were talking about. Surprised that he didn't know what had happened in Jerusalem, the two men told him about Jesus dying on a cross and shared their memories of his life.

* As the third disciple, finish the story by describing whom Jesus wants to join on the road today – people and nations of our time who may know disappointment and disillusionment.

At the beginning of the Eucharist, there is an opening procession and a kind of invitation to join in. This is followed by a moment to look at our lives: our lack of hope, our short-term goals, our stumbling on the road. Members of the assembly recognize their limits, saying, "Lord, have mercy." They recognize their need to open their hearts to welcome and share the Word and the Body and Blood of Christ.

The proclamation of the Word:

> *Then [Jesus] said to them, "Oh, how foolish you are, and how slow of heart to believe all that the prophets have declared. Was it not necessary that the Messiah should suffer these things and then enter into his glory?" Then beginning with Moses and all the prophets, he interpreted to them the things about himself in all the scriptures.*

Jesus breaks open the Scriptures and reveals their meaning to the two disciples. He may have reminded them of Moses leading the Israelites out of Egypt and into freedom (Exodus 13:17-22; 24:3-11) and the long march of people throughout the ages who were waiting for the Messiah. Each year, in fact, Jewish people celebrate the Passover by remembering the liberation from Egypt and the sealing of the covenant with God. This time of remembering the wonders God has done for God's people is found in the Passover meal or *seder*.

- As the third "disciple" on the road to Emmaus, which word of hope would you like to bring to people on the journey today?

In each eucharist, we listen to the Word of God as a word of hope for our time. This liturgy of the Word includes readings from the Old Testament and the New Testament, the proclamation of the Gospel and the homily.

Bread, broken and shared:

> *As they came near the village to which they were going… [Jesus] went in to stay with them. When he was at the table with them, he took bread, blessed and broke it, and gave it to them. Then their eyes were opened, and they recognized him; and he vanished from their sight. They said to each other, "Were not our hearts burning within us while he was talking to us on the road, while he was opening the scriptures to us?"*

Jesus had given them a sign. At this sign, they recognized him: the one they thought was dead was alive! How can such a leap of faith be possible? How can this sign continue to speak to us today, after 2000 years?

- What are some signs, some evidence, of the loving presence of God in the world today?

In each eucharist, we break bread in memory of Jesus. In each eucharist, Jesus gives us a sign: "Take and eat; this is my body. Take and drink; this is my blood."

Sent forth to proclaim the Good News:

> *That same hour they got up and returned to Jerusalem; and they found the eleven and their companions gathered together. They were saying, "The Lord has risen indeed, and he has appeared to Simon!" They they told what had happened on the road, and how he had been made known to them in the breaking of the bread.*

Filled with joy, the disciples went to tell the others the Good News. Jesus was there among them; the love of Jesus gave meaning to their lives. They couldn't keep their joy to themselves.

- What can we do to spread the Good News today? What can we say to others we meet on the road?

It is the time of sending forth, the time for the blessing that sends Christians out to share, to announce the love of God, to do something for others.

THE POOR: OUR TOP PRIORITY

In search of justice
and solidarity

salt and light

An invitation from John Paul II

Many people are wounded by life: they are excluded from
economic progress, and are without a home, a family, a job;
there are people who are lost in a world of false illusions, or
have abandoned all hope.

(Message of the Holy Father for WYD 2002)

This time, because Jesus' call in favour of the poor cannot wait, we
will begin with "Open the Bible":

Open the Bible

*"Come, you that are blessed by my Father, inherit the kingdom
prepared for you from the foundation of the world; for I was
hungry and you gave me food, I was thirsty and you gave me
something to drink, I was a stranger and you welcomed me, I
was naked and you gave me clothing, I was sick and you took
care of me, I was in prison and you visited me... Truly I tell you,
just as you did it to one of the least of these who are members of
my family, you did it to me."* (Matthew 25:34-36, 40)

These words are from Jesus' statement on the last judgment. They
shake us up and invite us to take action. They also bring hope. Today,
disciples of Jesus continue to bring liberation and show solidarity to
those who need it most: prisoners, the sick, and the poor.

* In your local community, how do poverty and exclusion reveal
themselves? Who are the *hungry*, the *sick*, the *prisoners*, the
strangers?

What can we do?

It is normal to feel helpless at first when we are confronted with human suffering and injustice. What can we do to combat unemployment, illness or malnutrition? Our feeling of helplessness at times turns into total confusion when evil and its consequences take on huge, perhaps even global proportions. What can we do in the face of war and terrorism, or the inexplicable horror that was September 11, 2001, in New York, Washington and Pennsylvania, or the violence in Palestine and elsewhere? And yet, when confronted by the "vast expanse of human suffering," in his book *Jesus Before Christianity* (Orbis Books, 1994), Dominican theologian Albert Nolan wrote: "My work is to discover what we can do about it."

* What do you think of this work of "discovering what we can do"? According to you, what can we do to promote justice and solidarity on earth?

John Paul II reacts to the terrorist attacks on the United States on September 11, 2001:

Yesterday was a dark day in the history of humanity, a terrible affront to human dignity. How is it possible to commit acts of such savage cruelty? The human heart has depths from which schemes of unheard-of ferocity sometimes emerge, capable of destroying in a moment the normal daily life of a people. But faith comes to our aid at these times when words seem to fail. Christ's word is the only one that can give a response to questions which trouble our spirit. Even if the forces of darkness appear to prevail, those who believe in God know that evil and death do not have the final say. Christian hope is based on this truth; at this time our prayerful trust draws strength from it. (John Paul II, General Audience, September 12, 2001)

Christian solidarity at the service of justice

At the heart of the Church's faith lies the unwavering conviction that we can do something to fight against hate, against blind self-centredness, against injustice. This conviction is founded on the faith that Jesus himself has in our capacity to love and to forgive despite all opposition:

> *"By this everyone will know that you are my disciples, if you have love for one another."* (John 13:35)

In *Ecclesia in America*, Pope John Paul II denounces "social sins" that are obstacles to the practice of justice and solidarity:

> The Church's social doctrine also makes possible a clearer appreciation of the gravity of the "social sins which cry to heaven because they generate violence, disrupt peace and harmony between communities within single nations, between nations and between the different regions of the continent". Among these must be mentioned: "the drug trade, the recycling of illicit funds, corruption at every level, the terror of violence, the arms race, racial discrimination, inequality between social groups and the irrational destruction of nature". These sins are the sign of a deep crisis caused by the loss of a sense of God and the absence of those moral principles which should guide the life of every person. (John Paul II, Post-synodal Apostolic Exhortation *Ecclesia in America* [The Church in America], 1999, no. 56)

Almost 20 years ago, during his 1984 visit to Canada, the Holy Father had already drawn from the Gospel urgent global applications of the values of justice and solidarity. In his homily in Edmonton on September 17 of that year, he encouraged the rich nations to do an examination of conscience concerning the plight of the poor countries:

> So it is that Christ the judge speaks of "one of the least of the brethren," and at the same time he is speaking of each and of all. Yes. He is speaking of the whole universal dimension of injustice and evil. He is speaking of what today we are

accustomed to call the North-South contrast. Hence not only East–West, but also North–South; the increasingly wealthier North, and the increasingly poorer South.

(...)

Nevertheless, in the light of Christ's words, this poor South will judge the rich North. And the poor people and poor nations – poor in different ways, not only lacking food, but also deprived of freedom and other human rights – will judge those people who take these goods away from them, amassing to themselves the imperialistic monopoly of economic and political supremacy at the expense of others.

A world under the influence

In order to discover what we can do to serve our brothers and sisters, we must first understand the world in which we live. Our societies are influenced by three major characteristics:

- on a political level, the difficult search for freedom and democracy,
- on an economic level, the powerful hold of global neo-liberalism,
- on all levels, the growing influence of communications technologies.

All societies are not affected in the same way, but all are affected.

Political power

Even though no one is against virtue, we often hear from various parts of the world that freedom and democracy are in trouble, that human rights are being flouted.

For example, we find that

– governments are influenced by the rich,

– the media manipulate the public,

– politics are often far removed from reality,

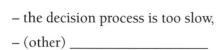
– the decision process is too slow,

– (other) _____

• What big or small things can we do to give freedom and democracy a chance?

Economic power

One of the major trademarks of the present economy, referred to as the neo-liberal economy, is that it tolerates some persons or societies accumulating enormous wealth while others remain mired in poverty. A quick overview of history shows that, while communism led to certain abuses, liberal capitalism leads to profound inequalities between the societies of the North and those of the South, as well as within countries. Left totally on its own, the effect of such a system is the continual deepening of the gulf between the rich and the poor.

• What do you think about the current economic system?

– I would like to understand better how it operates.

– We can't do anything about social inequality.

– These problems and issues are too big to deal with.

– It would take the involvement of a lot of people to bring about change.

– I want my place in the sun.

– I'm not really interested in politics.

– I want to do my share in my local community.

– *Other reactions:*

_____

Media power

Increasingly, a lot of information is circulated around the planet at incredible speed. The public is over-exposed to the media. Being informed is great. It stimulates one's intelligence, creativity and commitment. But the power of information has its snares and pitfalls. Here are two:

– It is not unusual for important news such as a famine ravaging a developing country or massive layoffs of employees to be shelved in favour of news of greater entertainment value, such as events in the career of a national or international star.

– Not everyone has equal access to information, entertainment and forums of debate. For example, only 20 per cent of the world's population has direct access to a telephone. Also, even in wealthy countries, not everyone has the ability or the financial means to make their opinion known in the media.

- Draw up two lists: the first showing the means of communication enjoyed by rich societies, and the second showing those accessible to the poor.

- With the help of these two lists, add a phrase to Jesus' statement on the last judgment (page 104).

The challenges of diversity

There are no doubt many other characteristics that could be applied to the societies in which we live. Among those that call for serious examination in the practice of justice and solidarity is the situation of Native and Aboriginal peoples in various countries, including Canada. Here is an excerpt of what John Paul II said in 1984 at a celebration at Martyrs' Shrine in Midland, Ontario:

> And today we are grateful for the part that the native peoples play, not only in the multicultural fabric of Canadian society, but in the life of the Catholic Church itself.
>
> (...)

This is truly the hour for Canadians to heal all the divisions that have developed over the centuries between the original peoples and the newcomers to this continent. This challenge touches all individuals and groups, all Churches and ecclesial communities throughout Canada.

- Can you identify in your local community traces of the characteristics mentioned above? Can you give one or more examples?

- Do you see other characteristics that could be added? If so, what are they?

"I was hungry…"

Let us now concentrate on situations of suffering, exclusion and poverty that exist in society. Whether or not these are part of our lives, we regularly witness heartbreaking human situations of this nature. Identify in the list of problems below those that you see around you.

- famine
- drug addiction
- violence
- suicide
- racism
- economic poverty
- sexism
- alcoholism
- prostitution
- gambling
- isolation
- other: _____

- What resources are there in your area to help those in need?

Seeking the causes

Solidarity with people living in situations of poverty, suffering or exclusion leads us to seek the causes of these situations. Identify in the list below statements that, according to you, sum up some causes of poverty, then add more in your own words:

– Poverty is inherited.

– Isolation is a vicious circle.

– Obsession with productivity writes off the least productive.

– Globalization of the economy creates pockets of poverty.

– _____

When we lift the veil on the causes of poverty, we quickly discover that a number of phenomena are intertwined. The problem is complex; simple explanations are not easily found. Above all, poverty is a social phenomenon that requires collective solutions.

• Can you think of ways to take concrete action against poverty, isolation or exclusion? What are they?

The ability of citizens to influence society helps them show solidarity. We all have the ability to bring about change, even if it is on a small scale. In the text from Matthew quoted on page 106, Jesus says that a simple glass of water given in his name is a great gesture. Feeling that we can change things helps us take action in society (see Suggested Activities, page 117).

The preferential option for the poor

In his statement on the last judgment (page 106), Jesus doesn't just draw attention to people who are suffering. He identifies with them; he joins with them:

> *"Truly I tell you, just as you did it to one of the least of these who are members of my family, you did it to me."* (Matthew 25:40)

These words of Jesus profoundly marked the lives of his disciples and continue to do so. An example of this can be found in the following excerpts from the address Pope Paul VI gave to members of the United Nations on October 4, 1965:

> What you are proclaiming here are the fundamental rights and duties of man, his dignity, his freedom …
>
> Your task is to see that there be sufficient bread on the table of humanity …
>
> But it is not enough to feed the starving; as well, each man must be assured a life in keeping with his dignity …

From Jesus to Paul VI, as from the prophets of the Old Testament to those of our times, the great heralds of the Word of God never stopped inviting to the "table of humanity" all who have been excluded or whose dignity has been wounded.

- "The surplus of the rich is the essentials of the poor," St. Augustine said.

- "Man is but the steward of his goods, not the owner," St. Basil said.

The Church has summarized this legacy and this project into a phrase filled with consequences: "the preferential option for the poor." Pope John Paul II talks about this in the Apostolic Letter on the new millennium, *Novo millenio ineunte*:

> Beginning with intra-ecclesial communion, charity of its nature opens out into a service that is universal; it inspires in us *a commitment to practical and concrete love for every human being* (…)
>
> Certainly we need to remember that no one can be excluded from our love, since "through his Incarnation the Son of God has united himself in some fashion with every person". Yet, as the unequivocal words of the Gospel remind us, there is a special presence of Christ in the poor, and this requires the Church to make a preferential option for them. (John Paul II, Apostolic Letter *Novo millenio inuente*, 2001, no. 49)

• How does the preferential option for the poor inspire you?

Great friends of the poor

Over time, in living out the Gospel, many great figures have shown the tradition of charity, of justice and of solidarity in the Catholic Church. The richness and diversity of their witness is limitless. We can learn by looking briefly at a few of these witnesses of the faith. Their holiness has been recognized and, in several cases, their witnessing gave rise to the founding of communities or to important work.

Martin of Tours (around 316–397)

Touched by the wretched state of a poor man, to whom he gave his cloak, Martin left the army, was ordained a priest and founded a monastic community at Ligugé.

Francis of Assisi (1182–1226)

Francis launched a vast spiritual movement based on the virtue of poverty, freely chosen and lived to the fullest. He also emphasized fraternal love and the importance of being close to the poor.

Vincent de Paul (1581–1660)

Vincent gave his whole life to serving the poor. He is the patron saint of charitable works.

Marguerite d'Youville (1701–1771)

Foundress of the Grey Nuns of Montreal, Marguerite was profoundly marked by the poverty she experienced as a child. She married, became a widow, raised her children on her own, then decided to dedicate her life to helping the poor in Montreal. With the help of three other women, and without any concern for race or language, she tended to unwed mothers, the elderly, orphans and others who were suffering from other forms of hardship.

Suggested Activities

Becoming aware of solidarity and justice

It isn't only great figures or well-known people who get involved with the poor. Countless men and women take part in a wide variety of causes to express their commitment to justice and solidarity. Here are a few possible options. Check those that correspond most to your interests, skills and concerns.

Opting for the poor by giving your time

- Offer your time to agencies that distribute food, clothes or other items.
- Offer to drive for agencies or for people who can't get around on their own.
- Perform small tasks (such as painting, cleaning or fixing) for those who can't afford such services.
- Teach language skills to a recent immigrant.
- Help people to understand and express their situation so they can stand up for their rights.
- Other: _____

Opting for the poor by advocating for them

- Join a reflection group that aims at better understanding society in order to find means to transform it for the better.
- Using the media, denounce unjust situations.
- Participate in walks or demonstrations for justice.
- Sign petitions denouncing abuse of power or injustices.
- Other: _____

Opting for the poor by being present to them

- Visit prisoners.
- Visit people living in shelters.
- Take the time to speak to someone who is begging on the street.
- Volunteer at agencies that are linked to your social concerns.
- Other: _____

Opting for the poor by sharing your possessions

- Help students who need books, supplies, etc.
- Share with agencies that support the poor, not only during the Christmas season but at other times of the year as well.
- Give money to agencies of your choice.
- Commit to buying more expensive consumer products rather than cheaper ones produced by workers who are exploited.
- Other: _____

Becoming involved in international solidarity projects

During the second half of the 20th century, the Church established a number of agencies dedicated to international solidarity, such as Caritas or, in Canada, the Canadian Catholic Organization for Development and Peace (CCODP or D&P). Recently, D&P developed an action plan called "Life is not for sale," which is aimed at preserving and sharing the natural resources of the planet. You can find this plan and more on the D&P Web site: www.devp.org.

Suggestions for Group Sharing

a) After the initial welcome, start the meeting by reading together "Jesus' statement on the last judgment" (page 106). Discuss the links between Jesus' statement and

– situations of poverty and suffering today

– the excerpts from John Paul II found in this Path.

b) Finish this biblical reflection by inviting a member of the group who has prepared in advance to speak on the love for justice that the prophets of the Old Testament demonstrated (see Appendix J).

c) Members of the group may wish to draw up a common action plan to be carried out in your area or at an international level (see Suggested Activities, page 117).

d) End the meeting with the prayer for WYD 2002 (page 17).

e) Choose a path, date, time and place for your next meeting.

APPENDIX J

The Old Testament prophets:
Passionate about justice and solidarity

The Jews grouped the books of the Bible under three titles: The Law, The Prophets and The Writings. The books of the Prophets therefore make up one of the three parts of the Old Testament.

The proclamations of the prophets were rooted in their direct and personal experience of God. This experience changed their perception of God, of life and of the world. Accordingly, they present a new and different understanding of God and of the chosen people. This is what explains their freedom of thought, the urgency of their proclamation and, often, their vehemence.

As well, the prophets were men rooted in their time, integrated and aware of the economic, political and religious stakes in their society. In an original manner, they reflect both their society and the God of this society, the dreams and sentiments of which they take on as their own.

For the prophets, the world of morality is incarnated in the social and political arenas, and therefore encompasses what, in our society, relates to social justice, civil rights and international politics. That is why they took very seriously the Code of the Covenant (Exodus 20:22–23:19), where the LORD lays out his demands: a society where right and justice prevail; and where the poor, the widow and the orphan have their place.

Sometimes the prophets spoke harshly. For example, the prophet Amos attacks the society of his time, which he sees as oppressive and exploiting. He denounces its social injustices: excessive fines, the doctoring of weights and measures, a corrupt legal system, people being forced into slavery for failing to pay minor debts. He denounces as well the hypocrisy of the superficial practice of religion in which the observance of rites takes precedent over the spirit of the LORD's commandments:

> *Hear this, you that trample on the needy,*
> *and bring to ruin the poor of the land, saying...*
> *[We will practice] deceit with false balances,*
> *buying the poor for silver*
> *and the needy for a pair of sandals...*
> (Amos 8:4-6)

That is why, through the prophet, the LORD demands justice:

> *I hate, I despise your festivals,*
> *And I take no delight in your solemn assemblies.*
> *Even though you offer me your burnt offerings and grain offerings,*
> *I will not accept them...*
> *But let justice roll down like waters,*
> *And righteousness like an ever-flowing stream.*
> (Amos 5:21, 22, 24)

Though Amos became known as the prophet of social justice, it can be said that all prophets, without exception, exposed the social injustices of their time as well as the hyprocritical cult-based practice of religion devoid of the love of the LORD , of obedience to his Word in regards to justice, of the sharing of goods and of respect of others. The prophets generally view this infidelity as the direct result of unfaithfulness to the LORD – of hearts that drifted away from God in favour of other gods and other laws.

(This text, by Christiane Cloutier, is published in Office de catéchèse du Québec [Catechetical Office of Quebec], *Justice et solidarité* [Justice and solidarity], Le cœur sur la main [Heart in hand] Collection, Montreal/Ottawa: Fides, Novalis, Médiaspaul, 2001, page V.)

TAKING A STAND

Being a witness of the Gospel

An invitation from John Paul II

> For a long time, salt was also used to preserve food. As the salt of the earth, you are called to preserve the faith which you have received and to pass it on intact to others. Your generation is being challenged in a special way to keep safe the deposit of faith.
>
> (…)
>
> Then you will be missionaries in all that you do and say, and wherever you work and live you will be signs of God's love, credible witnesses to the loving presence of Jesus Christ. Never forget: "No one lights a lamp and then puts it under a bushel" (*Mt* 5:15)!
>
> *(Message of the Holy Father for WYD 2000)*

Let's be honest: speaking about our faith in Jesus Christ is not easy! The spiritual life is often considered to be private. In addition to this, we may be afraid of imposing our beliefs on others; of being misunderstood; of being perceived as not being up to such a mission. And yet, if no one were to share the Gospel, how could anyone be touched by this Good News? Does it make any sense to keep our faith to ourselves? That would be like turning on a lamp only to hide it in a closet.

This becomes a real issue. How can we truly bear witness to the Gospel and yet avoid claiming to be better than others? How can we share our faith without undermining others' freedom of religion? This theme may prove helpful in resolving these issues.

- Read the following statements and check the ones that reflect your views even a little. Do not hesitate to add new ones.

_ "Proclaiming the Gospel sounds a bit like what a preacher does…"

_ "It is not through words, but through actions, that we can spread the Gospel."

_ "In order to speak about the Gospel, one should have studied the Bible."

_ "Share my faith in Christ? That doesn't bother me at all."

_ "Share your bread, it decreases; share your faith, it increases."

_ "All religions are equal… Why should we try to spread ours?"

_ "Bearing witness to Jesus is an integral part of Christian life."

_ "I can't find the words to express my faith."

Bearing witness to God: a path to freedom

When we have good news to tell, we tend to say, "Guess what! Something just happened in my life… in our lives…." We do not feel that we are bothering people when we have exciting news.

When we find a topic or field fascinating, whether it be computers, fashion, the arts, sports or current events, we can discuss it for hours without getting bored.

And yet we often feel uncomfortable speaking about Jesus, even if he is important to us. But what if our shyness were to prevent others from finding the meaning or freedom for which they are longing in their lives?

• What challenges do we face when we talk about Jesus Christ?

• Where do these challenges come from?

> "Modern man listens more willingly to witnesses than to teachers, and if he does listen to teachers, it is because they are witnesses." (Paul VI, Pontificate from 1963 to 1978, Apostolic Exhortation *Evangelii nuntiandi* [On Evangelization in the Modern World], 1975, no. 41.)

Here are five stories for you to read. They are all a little different, but they all speak of the benefits of witnessing to faith. It's up to you to see if you can find reasons in these stories to share your own faith, your own values, your own beliefs with others.

Sebastian's story

"What happened?"

Today, Sebastian is emerging from a long tunnel of fear and despair, and he shares with others the good news that he has come back to life. As a teenager, he found shelter in the "paradise" of hard drugs, not realizing that he was on the way to a "descent into hell." At age 19, he began to suffer terribly. He did not want to die, but death appeared more and more like the only way out of his pain: he felt like the only future that existed for him involved his dependence on drugs.

At the age of 23, Sebastian went back to school. He now works part-time and is learning to live in society. This is new for him. How did it happen? Sebastian met other former drug addicts who had gotten off drugs and who convinced him that it was possible to come back to life. No one forced Sebastian to enter this group or to stop taking drugs. It was by acknowledging his misery and noticing small miracles happening in other people's lives that he became convinced that recovery was possible for him, too. This liberation did not happen by magic. The witness of others gave him hope, but he needed – and still needs – to work hard to stay on track.

Sebastian gives his own testimony: "Getting off drugs was not easy for me. I kept falling back into my old habits. I had to ask for help from others and from God. (…) With others, I also learned to entrust myself entirely to a loving God whom I can still barely define. I find new strength in abandoning myself to someone who loves me and will never let me down. Nothing happens by magic, and I know that I cannot use God to satisfy all my needs. I am accountable for my actions. But I know that God's friendship will never fail me and, when I blame myself, God never stops looking at me with love."

- How do you feel after hearing Sebastian's story?
- Name some people who inspire you by their actions. How do they affect your life?

Sylvia's story

"See how they love one another..."

Sylvia is a student who leads a rather organized life, without any major problems. However, she wonders about the meaning of life and death, love and hate, employment and unemployment... In short, she asks herself extraordinary questions that ordinary people carry in their hearts. A kind of weariness exists in her, a feeling of emptiness, an impression that she was meant for something greater than what she has known up until now.

One day, she finds out that her friend Joanne belongs to a youth movement whose members meet regularly to share the Gospel. Intrigued, she asks if she can attend a meeting. She is amazed by what she finds there: happy people sharing their laughter and joy, who help each other in difficult times, who are open to loving and trusting others. Sylvia tells her friend: "I can't say whether I believe in your God, but I want to find the joy that lives in you! Can I join your group?"

- Have you ever had an experience like Sylvia's?
- What would you tell Sylvia about your experience?

Stories from Angola and Romania

"He spoke about forgiveness... she spoke about her Church..."

The third story is from the prayer vigil for WYD 2000:

"During the prayer vigil, there were some youth with physical disabilities and others from poor or war-torn countries on the balcony near the Pope. They were able to take part in this event because of the solidarity of WYD participants who gave money to cover their travel expenses. The WYD cross was like a symbolic spectator to the witnessing of the youth that alternated with great artists from around the world.

Domingos, a young guy from Angola, spoke first. He talked about forgiveness. The war has been going on in his country for 25 years. His parents died before he could even get to know them. His oldest brother became the head of the family, but then he was killed. Domingos told us how he found the strength to forgive his brother's killers and to pray for them.

Then a Romanian spoke. She is part of the Byzantine Catholic Church, which is being persecuted by the communist regime in her country. She talked about how hard it is to take part in prayer gatherings in secret, because they are forbidden. She even told us about an ordination that had to take place secretly: there was only the bishop, the future priest and two other people."

—*Author unknown*

The story of Philip and the Ethiopian traveller

"...he proclaimed to him the good news about Jesus"

The fourth story is found in the Bible. A passage from the Acts of the Apostles tells the story of an Ethiopian traveller who was coming back from a pilgrimage in Jerusalem. Sitting in his chariot, he was reading the prophet Isaiah. Then his path crossed Philip's...

> Then the Spirit said to Philip, "Go over to this chariot and join it." So Philip ran up to it and heard him reading the prophet Isaiah. He asked, "Do you understand what you are reading?" He replied, "How can I, unless someone guides me?" And he invited Philip to get in and sit beside him.
>
> (...)
>
> The eunuch asked Philip, "About whom, may I ask you, does the prophet say this, about himself or about someone else?" Then Philip began to speak, and starting with this scripture, he proclaimed to him the good news about Jesus. (Acts 8:26-35)

The Ethiopian traveller, after asking Philip for baptism, "went on his way, rejoicing."

* Do you know, on the roads of today, any "travellers" who are searching for meaning? What would you tell them?

The story of Pier Giorgio Frassati

A wonderful witness of the Gospel

The fifth story is one of a lifetime devoted to the service of the Gospel. Pier Giorgio saw Jesus in the poor. When a friend asked him how he could stand going into the filthy places he visited as he served the poor, he answered: "Remember that it is Jesus that you are going to visit: I see, around the sick and the poor, a special aura of light which we, the rich, do not have."

To learn more about the life and witness of the young layman Pier Giorgio Frassati, read his story in Appendix K.

* Do you know of any modern witnesses to their faith? How do they inspire you?

How can we express our faith?

"Let us proclaim the mystery of faith," says the priest during the Eucharistic Prayer. The assembly answers: "Christ has died, Christ is risen, Christ will come again." What an incredible statement! This is something: believing that Jesus is alive in this third millennium, and trusting in him. This statement could change the course of history and transform the face of humanity!

But we do not necessarily find the right words to express and remember this overwhelming mystery. How can we find the words to make the Word of God available to all, to adapt it to the real-life situations of the young and the not-so-young?

Resolving our faith issues

It is hard to talk about the Good News and to be at ease doing so if we have not dealt with our own issues. First, each of us has to enter into ourselves and, in all honesty, tell ourselves what kind of faith nourishes us, influences our choices and leads us to action.

*   Take time to write your profession of faith:
    "I believe…"; "I believe in…"

Letting ourselves be evangelized

Our faith has a community dimension. It draws on the faith of the Church. If we want to find the right words to express our faith, it is important to let ourselves be taught and evangelized in order to better grasp the meaning of faith. Together, and with the help of a guide, we can confront our faith in the Gospel and discover what it means. The members of the first communities have done so before us: "How can I [understand], unless someone guides me?" the Ethiopian traveller asked Philip.

Contrary to popular opinion, this teaching, called "catechesis," has something to say to young people as well as to adults. Is that surprising? No, because today, faith is not automatic. Not long ago,

salt and light

almost everyone in our society was born into a Christian family. Children learned about their faith in the same way as they learned to walk. They were given catechism classes, while adults were seen as no longer needing to be catechized. The general conclusion was that catechesis was for children. In our time, however, catechesis is more than ever seen as being for everyone, of every age.

Pope John Paul II talks about this in his apostolic letter on the new millennium:

> To nourish ourselves with the word in order to be "servants of the word" in the work of evangelization: this is surely a priority for the Church at the dawn of the new millennium. Even in countries evangelized many centuries ago, the reality of a "Christian society" which, amid all the frailties which have always marked human life, measured itself explicitly on Gospel values, is now gone.
>
> (…)
>
> We must rekindle in ourselves the impetus of the beginnings and allow ourselves to be filled with the ardour of the apostolic preaching which followed Pentecost. (John Paul II, Apostolic Letter *Novo millenio inuente,* 2001, no. 40)

- How could you let yourself be evangelized and catechized?

Evangelizing

The first disciples threw themselves into the adventure. They shared the Good News throughout the world. Some people, like the Ethiopian traveller, were open to hearing the Gospel. Others weren't; the disciples at times encountered opposition and major obstacles. Peter and Paul had their share of these, yet nothing could stop them. They persisted in their mission, moved by passion and an unshakeable faith.

Today, there are still witnesses; sometimes they are called missionaries. You may know of some. These are people who dare to take a stand and to make their beliefs known. They are people who join social movements to denounce unacceptable situations of injustice and poverty, or who, discreetly but directly, influence their environment. Evangelization requires people of all ages to work at "humanizing" the world by relying on the unconditional love of God, as Jesus did – and, like him, by totally respecting people's freedom. This is a passionate task that requires hands and feet, as Pope John Paul II says:

> This passion will not fail to stir in the Church a new sense of mission, which cannot be left to a group of "specialists" but must involve the responsibility of all the members of the People of God. Those who have come into genuine contact with Christ cannot keep him for themselves, they must proclaim him. A new apostolic outreach is needed, which will be lived as the everyday commitment of Christian communities and groups. This should be done however with the respect due to the different paths of different people and with sensitivity to the diversity of cultures in which the Christian message must be planted, in such a way that the particular values of each people will not be rejected but purified and brought to their fullness. (*Novo millenio inuente,* 2001, no. 40)

- Is proclaiming the Gospel possible? Under what conditions is this possible?

We are collaborators with God

We could say much more about evangelization and catechesis. Let us finish by simply recalling that this "work" is above all the work of God, in which we must collaborate.

> *"I planted* [Paul says], *Apollos watered, but God gave the growth. So neither the one who plants nor the one who waters is anything, but only God who gives the growth.* (1 Corinthians 3:6-7)

Proclaiming the Gospel sometimes doesn't seem to have concrete results. This is normal: the fruits of evangelization do not mature in one day; more often than not they grow to maturity without our knowing it.

Suggested Activities

- Watch the film *The Mission* (1986), staring Robert de Niro and Jeremy Irons:

> In the 18th century, Spain and Portugal were fighting over the territories of South America. The victims of this economic and military conflict were, of course, the native peoples of the lands. The native peoples nevertheless find allies in a Jesuit priest and his companions. Together they build an amazing Christian community that the economic, political and even religious authorities do not look on favourably.

– What kind of reflections on the joys and challenges of evangelization does this film inspire in you?

- Offer your services to a charitable organization that helps people in need, or do something to make people in your work or home environment more aware of the dignity of the human person.

- Find out about joining a group or movement whose members wish to be evangelized and to be witnesses of the Gospel, or form such a group with the help of some friends.

- Find out about signing up for a course to learn more about your faith, in a parish or elsewhere (catechetical sessions, courses on the Bible, etc.).

- Offer your services to accompany children, teenagers or adults who are preparing for initiation into the Christian faith, or who are preparing to celebrate a sacrament for the first time.

Open the Bible

Concerned about the need for evangelization, the bishops of several countries emphasize the necessity of "proposing" a faith. To propose is not to impose. Proposing does not mean that one should remain inactive, either. Thus, this invitation from Jesus:

> *"Go, therefore and make disciples of all nations, baptizing them in the name of the Father and of the Son and of the Holy Spirit, and teaching them to obey everything that I have commanded you."* (Matthew 28:19)

In the same breath, as a pledge of support for their mission, Jesus adds:

> *"And remember, I am with you always, to the end of the age."* (Matthew 28:20)

- What part could you play in this mission that Jesus entrusts to the Church?

Suggestions for Group Sharing

a) After the welcome and meditation time, invite members of the group to do one or more of the following:

- Comment on one of the five stories from pages 126 to 130.

- Summarize their own story: "What triggered in me the desire to make room for God in my life? What triggered my desire in the Gospel?"

- Share a part of this journey that particularly attracts their attention, and explain why.

b) One person can summarize the testimony of Pier Giorgio Frassati (see Appendix K) and explain why, according to him or her, this man was named a patron saint of World Youth Day.

c) Choose one of the Suggested Activities (page 135) and do the activity (or prepare to do so) together.

d) Close with the prayer for WYD 2002 (page 17).

e) Choose the path, date, time and place for your next meeting.

APPENDIX K

Pier Giorgio Frassati (Italy, 1901–1925)

Pier Giorgio Frassati was born in Turin (Italy) on April 6, 1901. His mother was a painter. His father, a notorious agnostic, was an impressive man: founder of the liberal newspaper *La Stampa* and influential in politics, he was named Senator and Ambassador of Italy in Germany. Pier Giorgio grew up with a younger sister, Luciana. Later he attended a Jesuit school, where he joined the Marian Sodality. He was given permission to receive communion daily, which was rare at that time.

He developed a deep spiritual life, which he shared freely with his many friends. The Eucharist and the Virgin Mary were the two poles of his prayer life. At the age of 17, he joined the Saint Vincent de Paul Society. He devoted most of his spare time to serving the sick and the needy, taking care of orphans and of the soldiers from the First World War. Pier Giorgio saw Jesus in the poor. When a friend asked him how he could stand going into the filthy places he visited as he served the poor, he answered: "Remember that it is Jesus that you are going to visit: I see, around the sick and the poor, a special aura of light which we, the rich, do not have."

Like his father, he was a strong anti-fascist militant, and never hid his political opinions. As a result, he often found himself in verbal arguments, first against the anti-clerical communists, and later against the fascists. Athletic and energetic, he was surrounded by friends, on whom he had great influence. Pier Giorgio chose not to become a priest, but to preach the Gospel as a layman.

Before he received his university degree in mining engineering, he contracted polio, perhaps – according to some physicians – from visiting the poor. After six days of agony, Pier Giorgio died at the age of 24, on July 4, 1925. His last thoughts were for the poor: the night before his death, he wrote to a friend, asking him to buy (and charge to his own account) medicine for a poor person whom he visited regularly.

At Pier Giorgio's funeral, the streets of Turin were filled with people who came to mourn his death. Most of them were unknown to his family: clergy, students, and the poor whom Pier Giorgio had served to the point of forgetting his own needs.

On May 20, 1990, Pope John Paul II beatified Pier Giorgio Frassati, whom he called "the man of the Beatitudes" and whom he had always admired. Frassati's life was a luminous illustration of the incarnation of the Gospel in a considerate love for the poor. His life was guided by the Spirit of the Beatitudes, and showed that giving up one's own desires to serve the Lord is a choice that is possible and that leads to happiness; that holiness is possible for all; and that only charity can give birth to hope and allow it to grow in a better world, in the hearts of the people.

BIBLIOGRAPHY

Canadian Conference of Catholic Bishops. *Catechism of the Catholic Church.* Author: Ottawa, 1994.

Catechetical Office of Quebec, *Justice et solidarité* [Justice and solidarity], Collection *Le cœur sur la main* [Heart in Hand collection], Montreal/Ottawa: Fides, Médiaspaul, Novalis, 2001.

Catechetical Office of Quebec, *Le cœur sur la main, Repères pour l'action bénévole dans les communautés chrétiennes,* [Heart in hand: Guidelines for volunteering in Christian communities]. Montreal/Ottawa: Fides, Médiaspaul, Novalis, 1998.

Catechetical Office of Quebec, *Rites et célébrations*[Rites and celebrations], Collection *Le cœur sur la main* [Heart in Hand collection]. Montreal/Ottawa: Fides, Médiaspaul, Novalis, 2001.

Encounters at Taizé, summer 1999. Theme: "The Covenant" (participant's notes).

John Paul II, Post-synodal Apostolic Exhortation *Ecclesia in America,* 1999.

John Paul II, Encyclical Letter *Evangelium vitae,* 1995.

John Paul II, Encyclical Letter *Fides et ratio,* 1998.

John Paul II, *Message of the Holy Father to the Youth of the World on the Occasion of the XVIth World Youth Day 2001.*

John Paul II, *Message of the Holy Father to the Youth of the World on the Occasion of the XVIIth World Youth Day 2002.*

John Paul II, Apostolic Letter *Novo millenio ineunte*, 2001.

John Paul II, Apostolic Letter *Orientale lumen*, 1995.

Mollat, M., *Les pauvres au Moyen Âge*[The poor in the Middle Ages]. Paris: Hachette, 1978, pp. 25-31.

Nolan, Albert, *Jesus Before Christianity.* Maryknoll, NY: Orbis Books, 1992.

Paul VI, Apostolic Exhortation *Evangelii nuntiandi*, 1975.